"Is it true?"
Bob's words were soft but pointed.
My own self-condemnation made me
want to run out the door and just keep
going, but I could never walk out on
those who meant so much to me.
"I drink a little during the day," I said
defensively. "Just a few drinks.
It's under control."
"Tell him everything," Mother urged.

SOMEBODY LOVE ME!

Sandy A. Atkinson
with Jan Markell

LIVING BOOKS
Tyndale House Publishers, Inc.
Wheaton, Illinois

Dedicated to . . .

My heavenly Father, who has said, "In the world you shall have tribulation, but be of good cheer, I have overcome the world" (John 16:30)

and

to my mother, who has been loving, patient, long suffering, and kind to me as a daughter.

They have both led me safely through the darkest storms.

I also want to express appreciation to my precious and faithful husband, Chip, who has understood and encouraged me, and has given his deep, tender, and unselfish love to me and our three children.

Sandy A. Atkinson

Library of Congress Catalog Card Number 78-68906
ISBN 0-8423-6065-4, paper.
Copyright © 1979 by Tyndale House Publishers, Inc.,
Wheaton, Illinois
First printing, December 1979
Printed in the United States of America

CONTENTS

PREFACE

I awakened from a drugged and restless sleep. The buckled leather straps that secured my arms and legs to the hospital bed had been tied too tightly. I remembered the struggle as the attendants had tied me in earlier that night. It had taken four people to strap me down. The night before, in the Psych Ward of North Memorial Hospital, I had reached for a razor blade to end the turmoil of my life. As the razor had pierced my skin, my desperate cry of anguish was heard by the entire floor.

It was still dark outside this morning, and the dim night light next to my bed just barely enabled me to see that it was 4:00 A.M. I couldn't move to push the button which would bring a nurse, and I didn't have the strength to call out. I would just have to wait until someone checked on me, probably during the 7:00 A.M. shift change. But that allowed me too much time to think. In the past my thinking and fears had been dulled by massive overdoses of Dexedrine capsules and alcohol. Before I admitted myself into the hospital I had been consuming sixteen Dexedrines and a quart of alcohol a day. I began taking Dexedrine at age eighteen in an attempt to keep my weight under control. I had gradually increased my dosage, and twelve years later I was taking one Dexedrine every hour. Now I lay strapped in a hospital bed, my mind and body shattered from such abuse.

Where did it all begin? Why did I have this nagging, relentless fear that I was of little use to anyone? Why this feeling of constant rejection, accompanied by an unending search for love and acceptance? I ached to truly belong, to fit in, to call someplace home.

That longing led to my desperate attempts to gain acceptance and love. The love I would find might last for a night, or a week, or a month, but it would eventually come to an end. Even my marriage had come to a disastrous conclusion. This had been the final blow in my twenty-nine-year struggle, which had prompted my desperate plea for help and hospitalization.

My mind drifted. For years now it had been difficult for me to carry a thought through, due to the overdoses of Dexedrines and alcohol. For the last few years I had ridden along on a chemical high. Even the prospect of a bleak future did not deter me.

My thoughts drifted back to my childhood, when my search really began. I relived the years, trying to piece the puzzle together.

ONE
A Shattered World

The pavement was cold and damp as I sat on the curb, stretching my neck to see the first sign of Father's diesel truck. It seemed a lifetime since he had left that morning, and my day was spent making the time pass quickly until we could be together again that evening. If Father was late I might spend many hours waiting on that curb, at the spot where I could best watch his truck coming into view.

What would Father bring home for me tonight? Each morning Mother packed a lunch for him, and each evening he brought home a different surprise for me in that lunch pail. The night before he had brought me two kittens which he named Whiskey and Bourbon. My six-year-old mind could never have imagined that those names would someday have significance in my life.

Mother and Father endured their marriage

for the first several years. They never raised their voices when I was near. But gradually Father began to drink and stay away from home more and more.

One Friday afternoon I assumed my usual post on the curb to wait for the red diesel to come into view. Minutes turned into hours, and Father still wasn't home. It began to rain late that afternoon, but I wouldn't leave my post. Toward evening Mother made me come home. Raindrops and tears streamed down my face together. My best friend hadn't come home. That was to be the first of many nights that Father stayed away.

Mother had many disappointments in life besides her marriage. She had been born to Jewish parents and raised in a liberal Jewish home in her early years. Later her family moved to a small town, and her parents faced the problem of finding her a good education. They learned that the finest school in the area was a Christian school, and friends strongly recommended that Mother be enrolled in its excellent program. Mother also learned about Jesus, but she kept the stories about him to herself.

My father, who was not Jewish, had little time for religion. He made fun of Mother, telling her she couldn't be a Christian and a Jew at the same time. Mother tried to tell me about Jesus, but I reacted with real disinterest. I was Father's little girl, and I wanted to be like him. He was big and strong and seemed to be self-sufficient. To maintain some peace at home, Mother grew more and more silent in her faith.

The pressures of life were closing in on Mother. She had suffered three miscarriages. Now Father stayed out late several times a week. When he was home he hurt Mother with a steady stream of unkind words. Perhaps her biggest hurt was that she felt I loved Father more than I loved her.

I slipped into a world of make-believe. With Father gone more often, I retreated to the little playhouse he had made for me in the backyard. But neither friends nor playhouse nor the pets he had given me were a substitute for being with him.

One afternoon my play-world was shattered with screams. I dashed from my playhouse to the front yard and stood in horror. Mother was standing in the middle of the street screaming incoherent words. Traffic darted around her or screeched to a halt. Confused motorists cursed her, then sped on. I later learned that Mother had wanted a car to run her down. The pressures of life had become more than she could bear. The shrill sound of a siren pierced the air. By now some people had stopped and tried to pull Mother from the street. The siren grew louder and the ambulance came into view. I closed my eyes and wept in confusion; and when I opened them, the ambulance was on its way and Mother was gone. A dazed group of spectators slowly returned to their cars and homes, and I was left standing in bewilderment.

That night the chilly night wind awakened me. For a moment I lost my bearings, then remembered I was at Mrs. Baxter's home sleeping on her porch. It was a tiny, enclosed porch surrounded by screened windows that couldn't be closed, so if it rained during the night, I would be soaked by morning. And since I always had a fear of enclosed places, my experience in Mrs. Baxter's front porch only added to that trauma.

Father had asked Mrs. Baxter to look after me while Mother was in the hospital. She was positively the world's shortest woman; at age six I could look her straight in the eye. But behind that four-foot frame was a bitter, angry woman. She ridiculed Mother, constantly telling me my Mother was crazy. I became her live-in maid, and while her three children lived a normal life, I cleaned and washed dishes continually.

But worst of all, I didn't get to see Father. I cried myself to sleep many nights, longing to hear Father's voice. At each ring of the doorbell or telephone my heart raced with anticipation. Mrs. Baxter only seized such opportunities to make fun of me.

"Face it, child, your father is off having himself a high time now that you two are out of his way."

I screamed in protest, "It's not true! Father is my best friend and he'll be here to take me home. I'm his very favorite. Just wait. You'll see."

"Your father is a drunk. And your mother is crazy. Did you know that? You know, you'll end up just like her . . . *crazy*, that is."

I dashed out of the house and ran for blocks until I fell to the ground in exhaustion and sat under a tree sobbing my heart out. I never wanted to go back to Mrs. Baxter's house.

"Father loves me best!" I protested loudly to a curious gray squirrel standing nearby. I wanted to befriend him and pour out my story to him, for it had been several weeks since I'd had a companion. But he scurried away to things of more importance.

As darkness approached I made my way back to the Baxters'. I was hungry and frightened to be alone in the dark. I kicked a can for a block, and as I rounded the corner to the Baxter home I looked up. There I saw it! Father's truck was in the driveway! He had come to take me home.

For a few months life returned to normal, as Mother had come home from the hospital and was doing well. It wasn't long, however, before Father began to drink again and to stay out late nearly every night. The inevitable happened. Mother had to return to the hospital.

"Please, Daddy, don't send me back to the Baxters'," I begged as he tucked me in bed the night Mother was taken back to the hospital. "Please. I'll do anything you say. Just don't make me go back."

I buried my face in the pillow, and Father saw how hurt his little girl was at having her home torn apart again. His strong but gentle arms reached out to comfort me. He held me for a long time that night, and as he tucked the covers over me, I felt sure I would not have to return to the Baxters'.

The next morning I met Sylvia; I'd never

seen a black person in our California suburb before. Sylvia was a large woman with piercing black eyes and a brilliant smile that fascinated me. She had a shrill voice that could probably shatter glass. Sylvia came to take care of me, and I quickly fell in love with her.

We became instant friends. She would scoop me up in her arms and love me to death. Father seldom came home when Mother was gone, and Sylvia was the only one who was ever able to comfort me in Father's absence. Each day she gave me a dime for ice cream, knowing it would deaden the ache I felt for Father.

Neighbors and relatives made fun of Sylvia, as it was unusual to have a black person in our all-white suburb. Relatives refused to enter our home. Or if they came, they wouldn't use our dishes in case they might get a plate that Sylvia had eaten on.

But Sylvia loved and forgave them all. She seemed to bear up under the absurdities of life, just filling the house with love for me and with good smells from the oven.

Sylvia came and went during the next two years while Mother continued to make trips to the hospital. Mother's frequent absence was seldom explained, but eventually she would come through the door with suitcase in hand. That meant my new friend Sylvia would have to leave, but it also meant Father would stay home more often.

I was eight years old, but I knew a great deal about being separated from those I loved.

TWO
"Father Won't Be Coming with Us"

"Hurry up, Sandy!" Mother urged. "Put your playthings in this trunk. If we don't hurry we may miss the train."

I was confused. Our weekend trip seemed to be more than a short vacation. Tension was in the air, and I hadn't seen Father in several days. I'd overheard a conversation a day earlier between Mother and a young couple, and it sounded as though Mother had sold the house to them. Added to the confusion was my fear that Father wouldn't be coming along. Perhaps I was stalling and delaying to give Father as much time as possible to show up. I finally asked the inevitable question, fear churning in my stomach.

"We will wait for Father, won't we?"

Mother hurried about the house and wouldn't look at me. I wanted her to notice my disappointment, but then I read a similar hurt in her own eyes.

"He won't be coming with us, Sandy. We're leaving him."

The churning in my stomach turned to frantic turmoil as I listened to Mother's words and read the look of finality on her face.

"Mother, what's happening? Where are we going?" Now I followed Mother around the house like a shadow.

"I simply won't go with you," I insisted. "If Father isn't coming along, I'll stay behind."

"We're going to start a new life," Mother said without breaking her pace around the house. "We'll stay with your grandparents in Minneapolis for a while and make a new life for us. We'll try to forget the past."

"But I don't want to forget!"

A cab honked impatiently as we made final preparations to leave for the train depot. I had to leave behind my playhouse and other memories of the man I loved so much. I felt nearly paralyzed with sadness and confusion. My world was falling apart and the most important person in my life was being severed from me.

As we traveled to the train depot I kept hoping that Father would show up after all. Perhaps he would appear with his suitcase to join us in a last-minute reunion.

My eyes frantically searched the train depot for my tall, handsome father. Everywhere people scurried and pushed and seemed to care very little about one another. Mother grabbed my hand and tugged at me as we made our way toward the train. My disappointment turned to fear and then terror. I just couldn't embark on this venture without my best friend.

As we boarded the train I took a seat by the window. I anxiously craned my neck down the long corridor, expectantly waiting. I hoped to see Father running toward us with a suitcase in hand! My heart raced. I knew Mother sensed my anxiety, but words were difficult for her now. She seemed to have a conflict of emotions: some sorrow and some resentment toward me and the situation.

Finally the train jerked and the finality of it all tumbled in on me. Father wouldn't make it after all. Tears streamed down my face and I buried my head in my hands.

"This isn't the end, Sandy. Actually, it's a beginning. We're going to start a new life . . . you and I. You will like Minneapolis. Your grandmother says that we can walk to the beach from her apartment."

She kept talking but I blocked out her voice. Why couldn't she love Father and make things work out even if it was just for me? Resentment began to build up within me to a boiling point. The train ride seemed endless. My eyes were swollen from crying and I didn't speak to Mother that first day. I refused to eat and I just stared out the window, looking but not seeing. I wanted no part of this life apart from Father. The hours dragged on as Mother and I sat in our mutual silence.

But on the morning of the third day I awakened to a new phenomenon. Snow! I'd never seen such a thing, and I got so excited that

I temporarily snapped out of my depression. Later that day we stepped off the train at our destination. Our new home was Minneapolis, Minnesota. The city was under several feet of snow and the intrigue of this new experience eased the pain of separation somewhat. But nothing could numb the hurt in my heart for very long.

We moved into a one-room apartment with Mother's parents. My "bedroom" consisted of a roll-away which was placed under the kitchen sink. Many nights I fell asleep to the arguments between my mother and grandmother. They fought over me frequently. Mother tried to defend my behavior and my grandparents couldn't understand why I sulked so much.

I was nine years old, but I had the bitterness and anger of an adult. I pouted and withdrew and sat out in the dark, smelly halls of our apartment building just to be away from people. I was sure that Mother and my grandparents didn't love me the way Father did. I decided to become as unlovable as I could to prove my point.

Every day I stole change out of my grandmother's purse. I bought candy or movie magazines to soothe my aching heart. I made a daily trip to a corner bakery to feed my face and further ease my hurt.

School was difficult for me. I couldn't concentrate and I spent most of the day staring out the window. My fourth-grade teacher grew more and more impatient, and one day in absolute frustration she took me into the coat room and pushed me up against a wall. She threw me with such force that my head banged against the wall and for moments I stood dazed, my head throbbing. She scolded me and shook her crooked finger at me. I didn't respond and this made her anger worsen. She grabbed my right arm and I felt her fingernails pierce my skin. She gave me two long gashes which began to bleed. Mother had never believed me when I told her of my struggle at school or of the impatience of my teacher. But when I got home that day she was finally convinced that I was struggling at school, and she agreed to meet with the principal. Three days later my teacher wasn't at her desk. I learned she had been dismissed for her behavior in the coat room.

My unhappiness led to compulsive eating and tremendous weight gains, and at age nine I faced the first episode in a lifelong battle with obesity. Much of my overeating was in secret, since I bought candy and bakery items with money I had stolen.

Summer came and I further consoled myself with food. My weekly visits to a child-psychiatrist ended when our finances ran out, but I was relieved. Besides, the psychiatrist was treating me for obesity caused by emotional problems while he himself was overweight.

Mother was very concerned about me and alarmed by my weight gain. She began to show me more love and planned weekly events to relieve my depression. She got me away from my grandparents more frequently, even if we just walked around the block. She tried to tell me about Jesus, but I wanted everything to be sanctioned by Father, so I reacted to Jesus with disinterest. She made an effort to draw me out with little gifts. Little notes greeted me in the bathroom, on a kitchen cupboard, or in dresser drawers. My depression eased a little by fall, but not my desire to see Father. I had no idea that the ensuing year would make the days of staring out the window in classroom 102 look good, for that fall I was sent off to a Catholic academy two hours away from Mother!

Why on earth was I being sent to a *Catholic* school? Father didn't believe in a God and Mother was Jewish, and I simply couldn't figure out how that could make me a Catholic!

Uprooted again . . . and now even Mother would not be near me! Mother finally explained that she had enrolled me in the Holy Angels Academy so that I could become a good Jewish Christian. All I knew was that if that meant more loneliness and separation, I wasn't the least bit interested!

Days and weeks dragged on endlessly, characterized by confusion, alienation and boredom. I was called the "Kosher Catholic," and spent endless hours in services spoken in Latin. I lived in a concentration camp-like dormitory with beds less than two inches apart. The windows were high above us and we couldn't see outside. I felt nearly abandoned and imprisoned and totally misunderstood by the staff of nuns. After a year "in exile," Mother Superior fully grasped my total despair and sent me home!

THREE
"Jesus-Killer!"

I entered another new school that fall. I anticipated the inevitable—starting over and making new friends. Both tasks were difficult for me. But I never dreamed I would soon become the brunt of the other children's ignorant prejudices.

The sixth-grade class was working on family trees the day I enrolled. I naively indicated that I was Jewish. Mother and my grandparents had always impressed upon me that I should be proud of that. My grandparents were proud that so many of the great men in history were Jews; and Mother always stressed the fact that God had used the Jews to give us the Bible and Jesus. For me, Jewishness would only mean trouble.

The day the other children found out, I suddenly became untouchable. Some of the kids went to the other side of the street when they saw me coming. They taunted me and yelled words I really didn't understand. I was called "Kike" and "Jesus-killer" and for the first several days was on the receiving end of stones thrown by some of the boys. I found even nastier notes awaiting me on my desk in the morning—with crooked, crossed lines on them which I later learned were Nazi swastikas.

I couldn't understand. Even though I wasn't interested in learning much about Jesus, I certainly didn't want to kill him!

Again those nagging feelings of loneliness and rejection returned. Was that all I should expect out of life? I came home in tears at the end of most days.

After one week of steady teasing, I came bursting through the front door into my bedroom. I buried my face in my pillow and pounded the bed in complete frustration. I heard Mother come to my bedroom door. She sat down beside me on the bed.

"Why am I a Jesus-killer, Mother?" I asked between tears.

There was a long moment of silence. "I had hoped that those days were over," Mother replied softly.

"What days?"

"The days of hating people because they're black, or Jewish, or just different, Sandy."

"So tell me why I killed Jesus!"

"You know the story of Jesus, honey. You remember seeing him hanging on a cross. Remember the pictures at the Academy? Some people think that the Jews made Jesus go to the cross because they were angry that he said he was a King and a God."

"So—I wasn't around when they killed Jesus!"

"People are ignorant, Sandy. Because our ancestors were guilty of rejecting Jesus, people make all of us pay. Not everyone, of course. But many people today are anti-Semitic. That means that they just don't like or trust Jews. Remember the way people treated Sylvia back in California? They made fun of her and said she was backward and ignorant. They were prejudiced and didn't bother to see the real Sylvia because they had their minds made up that she was different and beneath them. Well, it's the same with their dislike for the Jews. It's something that has been handed down from generation to generation, and they don't bother to look into it. They've been told that Jews have all the money and that they'll cleverly take money from them. People just don't trust the Jews. And if they use the Jesus-killer trick, they get a lot of people on their side."

"I'll go back to the academy before I'll go back to this school, Mother."

"Sandy, it will blow over, you'll see."

I rolled over and looked at Mother. "Mother, if I could go and be with Father a while, no one would have to know about this whole Jesus thing. Father's ancestors didn't kill Jesus, and Father doesn't even believe in him."

"We'll see, Sandy." A pensive look came over Mother's face, and she left the room.

Mother's love was about to be divided. She

told me that she planned to marry Leonard Levitan, a strikingly handsome Jewish man. Almost as handsome as Father! I could tell we weren't going to get along. I couldn't really blame him for not liking me right away . . . I was simply not a likable person!

Leonard allowed Mother to believe in Jesus, but made it clear that it would make him happy if I attended Hebrew school. In a desperate attempt to unite our family, I enrolled in Hebrew school, only to be asked to leave some weeks later. My attitude those weeks in class had been characterized by restlessness, rebelliousness, and boredom. More than once I had verbally insulted the Rabbi because of my own inner desperation.

All this despair drove me further to food, and at age thirteen I already tipped the scale at 170 pounds.

FOUR
Becoming a Woman

I entered high school at Washburn High in Minneapolis. Since I was physically mature for my age, I began to get a restored self-image because the other kids thought I was attractive. But keeping my weight down was an around-the-clock struggle.

In high school I met Brenda, and her friendship catapulted me into the mainstream of the young Jewish community. It wasn't easy for me to break into the subculture, for I was the only one who did not come from an affluent home.

But the feeling of acceptance by my new circle of friends created a new boldness and creativity in me. I pursued painting with water colors and won a city-wide award in a contest with hundreds of other high-schoolers.

I pursued music and became the lead singer in a pop group. All of the kids in it were seniors except me.

I took an interest in writing and again excelled and became editor of the school paper.

My life completely changed, and few knew the joy I felt at my newfound accomplishments and my increased self-confidence. Previously, the only ability I ever had was to gain weight quickly and easily.

Mother encouraged me to excel, and Leonard finally left me alone. He even seemed to be proud to have me as a daughter when I accomplished good things.

I ran for "Miss Richfield" while in high school, and came in as runner-up—it was one of my few high school endeavors in which I did not come out on top.

At this point, I determined to acquire Bob Abrams as a boyfriend. Every girl in school was in love with him. My friend Brenda pointed him out across a room, and though we hadn't yet met, I knew he was what I wanted. He was sixteen going on thirty. From a distance I admired his confident walk and his six-foot frame. He was going places and he knew it. I was told he broke all the girls' hearts, and that he'd do the same to me. But I knew differently.

When Bob Abrams came into my life I finally knew I had met someone who could ease the ache in my heart to be with Father. Bob made me feel special. For once I was the most important thing in someone's life, and for once I felt secure. His family also loved and welcomed me. It was my home away from home, and I never felt in the way.

Bob was a hard worker and he helped out

in his family's delicatessen every day after school and on weekends. We saw each other during lunchtime at school, and he always made it a point to take Friday night off so we could be together. Each night he called me from the deli, but Leonard would not let us talk for more than three minutes. We crammed a lifetime's worth of conversation into those three minutes!

It had been impossible for me to risk my feelings with a man before because it had always meant rejection and hurt. But I knew this was different. I felt safe and cared for with Bob; consequently, my whole countenance changed. I was a woman who was loved.

If only I could have stopped the clock on those high school years. I was racing toward the dawn of a twelve-year living, walking nightmare.

FIVE
A Not-So-Quiet Diet

After graduation from high school I entered
nurses' training at Glenwood Hills Hospital in
Minneapolis. Bob and I planned to marry when
he finished school. Our study and work sched-
ules allowed us little time to see each other, and
thus the haunting insecurities of the past drove
me to the comfort I had always found in food.

Food solved so many of my problems, while
causing countless new ones. Food soothed
loneliness, boredom, frustration, and anger.
Food represented love and security. Food
became my constant companion and my best
friend. But the realization that I had lost control
over my eating brought real terror to my mind.
The pounds and inches kept increasing, forcing
me to revamp my wardrobe every few months.
Food became my purpose for living. I kept
raising the ceiling to my limit before I called it
quits to the compulsive eating. I said I would

allow myself to hit 140 pounds, then stop. I moved it up to 150, then 160. When the scale passed 170 and I moved into my third uniform size in five months, I panicked. At one unguarded moment I caught a glimpse of myself in a full-length mirror. I was repulsed by my 5'4" body bulging everywhere it shouldn't and crowding out the uniform.

I was desperate. I saw my whole future washed away because of my uncontrollable desire for food. I tried every gimmick available in order to lose. A diet never lasted more than an hour before I would hit the junk food again, like an addict returning to his needle.

I was the perfect target for Satan, who came to me as an angel of light through a friend. She introduced me to the wonder of Dexedrine, the chemical cop-out, which lured me by the promise of fast weight loss. It was a sure thing, and I saw it as my gateway to happiness. And to me, happiness was measured by having a slim figure and being loved by a man.

Dexedrine is the most popular form of "speed" used today. It makes depression vanish in seconds and, when used without caution, sends one on a high that might last for days. Sleep is impossible when the dosage is abused, and the thought of food can be erased from the mind for days.

I took only one capsule and the insecurities of the past and present faded away. The irony to chemical highs is that one feels free and liberated, when he is in fact enslaved. After I took the Dexedrine that morning, food was totally out of my mind and I breezed through lunch hour without a single hunger pang. I didn't even have an emotional need for food.

So why not double the pleasure? The next day I doubled the dose and took two capsules, and the third day I doubled it again and took four. A week later I was taking eight Dexedrine capsules a day and my friendly supplier cut off the flow of pills. But by then I had free access to them from the hospital medical cabinet. I would make the most of that situation.

Taking eight Dexedrines a day now, I neither had to sleep nor eat. Instead, I coasted along chemically revved up, feeling for the first time in my life not an ounce of fear or depression. I was one of the better students in training. I was the most meticulous, and I finished my duties hours before I left the floor. With the stimulation of eight pills a day, there was no limit to what I could accomplish in a short period of time. I became carefree and I joked nonstop with everyone.

I got down to two meals a week and the pounds rolled off. I was also down to less than an hour of sleep at night. I roamed from room to room of my classmates and killed time with them all night. When one went to bed, I simply moved down the hall and visited with another. When it began to get light out I would lie down for an hour or so, and then get up, ready to lick the world—that is, as long as I popped another Dexedrine and continued to take them throughout the day.

I felt so good that I had no idea how I was

abusing my body. Dark circles formed under my eyes that exist to this day. I didn't allow my body to repair itself through sleep. I was nutritionally starving myself, and the lack of proper vitamins in my diet began to show. But even the unpleasant side-effects of vitamin loss didn't stop me, for I felt carefree as I headed toward my desired weight of one hundred pounds. Those nagging insecurities of life just washed away.

I developed sores in my mouth, and I noticed that I bruised easily. My skin grew dry and flaky and I had skin eruptions frequently. At first headaches were just a nuisance, but as the weeks wore on they became severe. My hair began to come out easily, and when I saw my first bald spot I put myself on an intensive vitamin program.

Bob was alarmed at the change in me. He was so caught up with school and work that I was sure he would believe me when I told him I was just on diet pills. Suspicion was evident in his eyes. He saw how my memory failed me frequently. I talked nonstop and rambled. My jokes became obnoxious and I could take nothing seriously. I was in high gear twenty-four hours a day.

Toward the end of nurses' training, I took one Dexedrine every two hours. The sky was the limit to what I wanted to do. As long as I was on the stimulant, I felt like Wonder Woman.

I decided I wanted to start married life with some money, so I left nursing and went into sales. With my new drugged personality I knew I could be a whiz-kid in that field. I joined the Hope Chest Company, selling items to engaged girls. Within months I shot to the top in sales. Soon I had twenty salesmen under me and I was on my way to big money. My weight was under control and I could work all night without sleep—if I was on the pills.

To my dismay I found that in spite of eight Dexedrines a day, I again began to gain weight. I knew that my body was building up a tolerance to them and that the dosage had to be increased. I would stop at nothing to put the brakes on any weight gain. I decided to take the capsules once every half hour to insure weight loss or control. The bottle of 1000 I had taken with me from the hospital was now nearly empty.

The pounds and the cares rolled away again. Sleep was impossible now that I was taking sixteen pills a day, and so I stayed up all night painting. I lost track of time and portions of the day blanked out on me. Fortunately I didn't have to punch a time clock, so no questions were asked when I was gone for a day or two.

Bob was very alarmed at my personality change. I did all the talking and changed subjects in the middle of a sentence. I slurred my words and forgot what I was talking about before I finished a sentence. The circles under my eyes were getting darker and I couldn't string Bob along on the diet pill idea much longer. I was restless and couldn't sit still even with Bob. I became dizzy from the overdoses and developed severe headaches.

I acquired a cough that lasted night and day for a week and finally had it checked out by a doctor. As he examined me he grew suspicious. He saw in me signs of an addict hooked on speed. He wrote out a prescription for the cough, then looked up at me over the top of his glasses.

"Young lady, you're in terrible shape. What is it you're taking?"

"Diet pills. Several a day." I don't know why I thought I could fool him.

"Diet pills wouldn't be doing what I see happening to your body," he stated with fatherly concern. "Your body is starved for the vitamins and nutrients it can only get from a balanced diet. I think you're taking speed. What kind?"

"Well, I take a Dexedrine now and then. It helps me cope, you know? It increases my sales and it gives me the personality I need. I know when to quit, though. Never take more than two or three a day."

"If you take one it's too many. Dexedrine is the most abused drug I know of. It'll send you to an early grave. Pretty soon your body may be beyond repair to have children. Do you want that?"

I felt the conversation had gone too far and I wanted out. "It will be all right. I can quit in a day if I have to."

I thought of asking him for a prescription to obtain more Dexedrine, but I realized such an attempt would be futile.

I turned to him as I reached the door to

leave. "Look, I appreciate your concern, but right now it's just very important that I keep my weight down. I don't think you can understand that. It means more to me than to most people, I guess. Maybe it goes back to my feeling unloved as a child because I was heavy. I can't let it happen again." I closed the door and left the office.

That night I paced the floor in my apartment. Where in the world would I get a new supply of the pills? I had enough for only three more days. I racked my brain trying to think of a connection. I thought of calling Bob, but I couldn't tell him that I was on anything other than diet pills.

I called some friends whom I thought might be able to steer me to a source. I learned that the going price for the quantity I needed was nearly $200 a month. I was stunned to hear it, and I felt I had really hit bottom. As I envisioned the forthcoming weight gain, I resolved to pay any price to prevent the scale from climbing. All turmoils of the past seemed insignificant compared to the sudden realization that unless I found a new source for the pills, my chemical high and my slim appearance might soon be shattered.

Two days later the bottle of pills ran dry. I prepared for work that morning, wondering how I would cope. My every thought was of finding a fresh supply through some miracle that day.

By mid-morning I knew I needed another capsule to get me through the next two hours.

The high was wearing off quickly—a feeling I hadn't known in over a year of continual chemical euphoria. I got up from my desk to leave the office, but caught my shoe on a rug. I toppled to the floor in pain, stunned and afraid of further delays in finding a source for the pills. But a way of escape was to me made for me.

I was taken to the company doctor that morning. I began to noticeably tremble on the way and attempted to explain to the young lady assisting me. My head felt like someone was striking a gong inside it, as I had hit my head on a desk as I fell. And I hadn't slept or eaten in two days. Depression circled me like fog—a depression from "coming down" off the Dexedrine.

Dr. Jacobson, the company doctor, saw me immediately. When I looked at him he reminded me so much of Father that I was sure he noticed my strong reaction. He checked out my ankle, which I had twisted, and put some medicine on the bruise on my head. He made some routine tests and checked my pulse and blood pressure. I knew I was about to be handed another guilt trip from the medical profession about abusing my body. I saw it written all over his face.

"You're on speed, aren't you?" he questioned, already knowing the answer.

I was frozen to the chair. Now word could get back to my employer and I would be dismissed.

"Don't worry, I'll keep a confidence," he

stated, sensing my fear. He sat in a chair across from me and seemed to look at me with concern.

"Well, I take a little speed now and then to control my weight. You know, maybe once a day or so," I said. It was like a rerun of the routine I had been through with the other doctor.

"Well, once a day might be OK. But a young lady like you with high blood pressure has to be taking more than one a day. It's my guess you're taking eight or more a day. Am I right?"

"Occasionally I take more."

"And it's my guess that part of your problem today is that you need a supply of speed. Am I right?"

What should I say? Could he help me, or would he turn me in?

Several seconds of awkward silence passed.

"Yes, I need a new supply. I'll pay any price. Could you give me a prescription?"

He was obviously impressed at the tension in my voice.

"I think I can help you, young lady. How many do you need?"

I was desperate; this could be my source. "Frankly, doctor, I need sixteen a day. I go through a bottle of a thousand in two months."

I waited for him to react but he didn't respond for several long moments.

"That's an expensive habit you have. I think you and I could work something out so it wouldn't cost you a thing. Not in dollars and cents, that is. Know what I mean?"

I didn't. I was confused and he saw my bewilderment and seemed amused.

"Let's just say that you would be returning a favor for a favor. You could come up here to my office, or we could meet on some neutral ground. You do a favor for me and I bring you a bottle of 500 Dexedrines. The next month we do it again."

It finally hit me and I couldn't respond. What was I getting myself into? I was so desperate I knew I had to accept his offer. I couldn't stand myself. I hated Dr. Jacobson for making the offer, but I knew I had to agree to the terms. I was painted into that proverbial corner.

He sent me out of the office with instructions on how to obtain a month's supply of the Dexedrine from his source. Before I could get a second month's supply, I would have to meet him and fulfill my part of the bargain. No cash involved—only the selling of my dignity.

As I walked down the stairs from his office I faced the realization that I was hooked on speed and that my life revolved around it. I was willing to go to any lengths to obtain it. Only the promise of downing another Dexedrine within the hour could numb that terrible realization.

SIX
Diabolical Daily Devotions

I became acquainted with a new intrigue at this point in my life. I was always fascinated by the supernatural and I found myself turning to the astrology column in the morning paper each day with real devotion. Soon I took the daily warnings and predictions very seriously and didn't even get out of bed until I read the daily horoscope and then planned my day accordingly. The daily predictions were frequently accurate, and the day it told me I would have an automobile accident I took special notice. That afternoon I hit another car coming down a parking ramp.

I knew there just had to be something about astrology that made it more than a game of chance, luck, or fate. I fit the Gemini description perfectly—outgoing, flamboyant, domestic, and eccentric! There was something about astrology that drew me like an insect into a spider web.

I knew what sign someone was just by talking to him for a few moments. I decided I couldn't trust anyone who wasn't a Gemini, Aquarius, or Virgo, and if someone who came into my life didn't fit one of those three groups, I dismissed him as a friend or acquaintance.

My astrology books became my "daily devotional" guides. Each day was carefully planned by the books. Social activities were scheduled for when the books said they were safe. I won others to this fascinating "science" with the greatest of missionary zeal. Astrology lingo was the first piece of conversation out of my mouth wherever I went. I put an astrology bumper-sticker on my car and gave away jewelry bearing astrological signs for gifts. Astrology quickly became more than a fascination—it became a way of life. And it was just another stepping-stone which allowed Satan to further control my life. It seemed that now the forces of evil moved in with greater intensity to further usher me into their diabolical kingdom.

SEVEN
Withdrawal

I was now nearly twenty and Bob and I had
been in love for five years. Bob's parents were
against our marrying before he finished school,
but we went against their wishes and were
married by a Justice of the Peace in a small
northern Minnesota town. However, we planned
to return to Minneapolis and live separately, not
telling anyone that we had married.

The idea worked for about three days and
then I missed Bob so badly I could think of
nothing else. Bob continued on with classes in
an ROTC program at the University of Minnesota. He also worked nearly full time at the
deli. Somehow we managed to spend time
together between those responsibilities. I was
angry with Bob, his parents, and life, and re-
sented always being second or third down the
line in priorities.

I grew suspicious that I had an ulcer. Along

with those symptoms I began to gain weight, in spite of sixteen Dexedrine capsules a day. I was alarmed especially at the weight gain, for I couldn't increase the dosage of the pills. The symptoms worsened and my weight kept climbing; finally it occurred to me that I could be pregnant. My suspicions were confirmed and more turmoil overcame me the day of the diagnosis. I remembered reading the warnings about Dexedrine directed to pregnant women. Even one capsule during pregnancy was discouraged. How could I manage sixteen a day and expect to have a healthy baby? I knew I had to get off the pills during the pregnancy, but was I prepared to pay the consequences? I was a coward and the thought of withdrawal symptoms sickened me. Now Bob would see me ill and I would have to confess to him my addiction to the pills.

I walked up and down the crowded streets of downtown Minneapolis for two hours that afternoon. Did I have the right to produce a deformed child because I didn't want to endure a week of withdrawal? Could I send someone into a lifetime of disability or retardation because I didn't want to be uncomfortable? I had to get off the pills quickly and protect the baby. I could always go back to them after the baby was born.

The pregnancy forced Bob and me to live together, and for this I was thankful. But Bob's parents insisted we have a Jewish wedding and they made plans for us to go through with a second ceremony. I knew I couldn't handle the pressures of the wedding apart from the pills; however, the day the wedding was over I determined to get off of them for the baby's sake.

Bob and I moved into a small apartment the day of the wedding, which we later learned was directly above a boiler room. The apartment turned out to be a sweat box with steam from the boiler constantly coming up through the floor and turning our home into a sauna.

We had had a lovely Jewish wedding; only Father's presence could have made it more beautiful.

It was nearly 3:00 A.M. as Bob and I sorted through some wedding gifts and looked back on the evening. I leaned back on the secondhand sofa his parents had given us. Bob came and sat beside me as we looked over our first effort at a home. It was a humble beginning to be sure, but I was so happy to have Bob with me that it didn't really matter now.

"Well, it's simple and basic," Bob said apologetically, "but what do you want from a part-time clerk at your local deli?" Bob winked at me and opened a wedding gift.

"We'll fix it up," I replied enthusiastically. "In a month I bet we won't recognize the place." I knew I wouldn't be in any shape to do any fixing up, nor did I care if we ever did it. It was a start and it was home, and I was sure we could fill the place with love.

"Bob, there is something I need to tell you." The urgency of my voice caused Bob to give me his immediate attention. My last

Dexedrine had been taken over two hours before and it would be my last one until after the baby was born.

"I haven't been exactly telling you the truth in one area. I was sure I could fool you about the diet pills. Well, you were so caught up in school and work I thought I'd keep something from you and you would never know. Have you suspected anything about them?"

Bob's face grew serious. "It has occurred to me that you're on speed. Is that it?"

"Yes. I've been taking Dexedrine for some time. I've taken as many as sixteen a day. But I've gotten so I can control my personality now and not always act so high. And yet I can feel good and keep my weight under perfect control. But I'm quitting, Bob, starting tonight. I'm quitting for the baby's sake, hopefully forever. The pills have been costing me over $100 a month."

Bob grimaced at the reality of the problem. "Why did you feel you had to keep it from me? Maybe I could have helped you come off them before this."

"I haven't wanted to come off them, Bob. The pills make me the kind of person I want to be—confident, witty, and good in sales. I can feel able to lick the world as long as I'm on them. They block out all insecurities. I've enjoyed every one I've taken. They're my method of coping in life."

"But you are quitting now. You must, you know." Bob's concern was for both me and the baby. His voice reflected compassion. I was sorry I hadn't brought him into the picture sooner; I'd felt so alone in my struggle with the pills.

"I'm quitting tonight, Bob. Two hours ago at the wedding reception I took my last Dexedrine. I just had to in order to get through the whole relative scene. You know I'm not really confortable around some of your relatives. But you saw how I breezed through, didn't you? It was because of the pills."

"So how did you keep yourself supplied with the pills?" Bob asked the inevitable question.

"I made a deal with the company doctor. I saw him once a month, and he gave me a bottle of 500. Normally that would have cost me a lot—over $100 at 25 cents a pill. But I must confess, Bob, it didn't cost me a thing as long as I returned a favor for a favor. I know you're disappointed in me. You should be."

"But it's over now, isn't it, Sandy?"

"Bob, I want it to be, but not only do I need the pills physically, I need them for the emotional trip they give me. You don't understand, I know. That's way I didn't want to tell you. The pills make me what I'm not. They make me fun and popular. They take away depression and guarantee I won't gain weight."

Bob kept in control and showed great compassion. His voice assured me that he wasn't going to add to my guilt feelings.

"I'll help you, Sandy. You're acceptable to

me. I fell in love with you when we were fifteen, and you weren't taking them then. I must have seen something about you I liked, and it was all *you*, without a chemically induced personality."

"Bob, I'm about to get very sick tonight. I'll be very sick for several days, coming down from the pills. I don't want you to stay home because I'm embarrassed to have anyone see me as an addict coming off the stuff. Please go to the deli in the morning and let me kick it alone. I'll be unbearably hard to live with for a while. I'm sorry to start out our marriage like this. You deserve better."

Bob didn't say anything but began to unpack a few things and seemed deep in thought. The signs of discomfort were beginning within me. I knew Bob had to get some sleep, for Saturday was a big day at the deli. We had planned no honeymoon as we needed the extra money so badly. I hoped that the worst of the withdrawal symptoms would hold off until after Bob left the next morning.

"If you want me to go, I will, Sandy, but I'd prefer to help you lick the problem. It's more important to me than the money I might earn in the next few days. Let me help you."

I went over and lay on the bed, staring at the ceiling for several minutes. I felt a cloud of depression envelop me, and I recognized it as the first sign that I was coming down off the pills.

"The best way you can help is to let me be alone a while," I said softly. My voice sounded defeated before I even started. I lay motionless, aware of every part of my body and the little discomforts that started to set in.

I pretended to fall asleep so that Bob could get some rest that night and not worry so much about me. The symptoms weren't severe yet, and four hours later Bob quietly left the apartment for the deli. I hadn't slept a moment during the night.

An hour after he left, the symptoms worsened. My head throbbed, making my childhood migraines seem insignificant by comparison. The depression closed in and was overwhelming. My moods had been so chemically controlled for two years that I couldn't respond without the drug. I sat on the edge of the bed weeping, full of fear and self-pity. My muscles ached and my bones felt brittle. I was afraid to move from the bed, for the sagging mattress was so soft that it cradled my body gently. Nausea was setting in, and when it eased up it was replaced by obsessive appetite. I ransacked the refrigerator, eating everything in sight, then went to the bed and felt the nausea return.

All day the symptoms worsened. I got the shakes and couldn't stop trembling for hours. Bob called every few hours and finally left the deli early to be with me. His presence only made me more uncomfortable.

I was haunted with thoughts of cheating and going back on the pills. I could have eased my agony by retrieving them from their hiding place. I made a secret vow to resume taking the pills after the baby was born. I was so frightened by the compulsion I had for food every time the nausea eased, that I vowed to take the Dexedrine the rest of my life to keep my weight and appetite under control.

That evening I took out my misery on Bob and shouted verbal abuses at him. Neighbors on both sides of our apartment came over to see what the chaos was all about, all of which added to my self-condemnation and guilt.

The physical and emotional symptoms continued and worsened well into the third day. Bob refused to leave, staying by my side, rubbing my back, and trying to be of comfort to me. The temptation to forget this whole self-righteous plan became an obsession.

By the fourth day I felt some relief, and that evening I was sure I had made it. I felt like I'd come out of some form of mental illness, as a degree of sanity returned to me. I was very grateful for Bob, because he patiently endured the ordeal with me and never left me after that first day. We both lay down on the bed utterly drained and exhausted. At last I drifted into a deep sleep—perhaps the first real sleep I'd had in two years, for I was finally free from the stimulant that had revved me so high that I needed neither sleep nor food to function.

Our son Mark was born and I don't think any woman could have been as happy as I. Not only did I have a lovely boy, but I had not yielded to that nagging voice that wanted me to go back on the pills during the pregnancy to stop the weight gain. The driving force behind that inner compulsion was powerful. Giving in to it had always been inevitable—but not this time.

And yet the sixty-five pounds I'd gained glared at me as I looked at myself in the mirror. My weight seemed to taunt me and sneer at me. I knew that a diet didn't exist that could help me lose it. It had to be the pills again.

But I had only a ten-day supply of the pills left over from before the pregnancy. I had to find a new source for the Dexedrine and my obstetrician would only give me a prescription for one a day. At that rate, I realized, I would use a two-week supply in one day in order to accomplish my goal of quick weight loss.

I visited other doctors and received small prescriptions for the pills. I juggled refills at various pharmacies so that I could get the quantity up. Within a week the other doctors caught on and cut off my supply.

Again I underestimated Bob's perception. I was sure he was caught up with school, work, and his new son, and that he wouldn't see the telltale signs that I'd gone back on the pills. The fact was, even the most unobservant person couldn't miss the clues: hyperactivity, lack of appetite, and the inability to sleep at night.

He was unusually quiet one night as he came home from the deli. He hardly said a word as he went through his usual routine, from the baby to the refrigerator to his books. He sat on the sofa with his books spread out before him on the floor. The silence was awkward.

"Something wrong?" I questioned.

"I'm just concerned about you. You're back on the pills."

"It's only because of my obsession for food," I said awkwardly. "I can't get it out of my mind for a minute without the pills. It's kind of a crazy circle, I guess—sometimes food is love to me; and yet when I'm heavy, I feel nobody could ever love me."

"So who needs to love you outside of me?"

Bob raised a valid question. I felt genuinely secure in his love.

"In two months I'll have this weight off. Then I'll quit again, for good. I give you my word. Help me get a two-month supply."

"How many a day?" he questioned. "No deal if it's sixteen a day. I won't stand by and watch you kill yourself."

"I'll cut it in half. Help me get five hundred capsules, and when they run out, I'll quit."

Without a reply Bob went to the phone and made three calls in an attempt to track down a supplier of the pills for me. A twinge of guilt stabbed me as I realized I had now involved the one closest to me in my continuing problem. And yet I could soothe my nagging conscience by reminding myself that I wanted the Dexedrine strictly to be more attractive for Bob. He was genuinely proud of me when I was slim. Nothing, in fact, so perfectly satisfied me as pleasing Bob in every way possible.

Bob paced the apartment as he impatiently sought a supplier for me. Because of their popularity, the Dexedrine kept going up in price;

but he finally located a connection for the pills. The price for five hundred capsules would be $120.

I kept my word to Bob only up to a point: I did drop down to one capsule every two hours rather than one every hour. But deep within me I still recognized that obsessive need to keep taking the pills well beyond my supply of five hundred capsules. Watching that limited amount dwindle shot real terror through me. I was even sure Bob would help me find an additional supply, but my fear in disappointing him haunted me further. More than anything I wanted a happy marriage; a marriage uncomplicated by my uncontrollable needs. I wanted Mark to grow up in a home free from any tension I might create due to my excessive need to be slim. And yet, I felt supernaturally chained to that need. It defied my pitiful attempt to logically figure it out. I generally gave up the attempt at analyzing the situation and just yielded to the nagging temptation to take another Dexedrine.

A month later Bob graduated from his ROTC program at the University of Minnesota. He hoped to enter the Army upon graduation. My underlying fear was that such a plan meant relocation, and relocation meant finding a new pill supplier. I was comforted in the belief that Bob would handle that dilemma when the time came.

For several anxious days we waited to receive our orders to report to an Army base. At last we heard that we were being sent to Oakland, California, less than twenty miles away from my father! In my wildest dreams I would never have hoped for Oakland! Now Father could see that his little girl had really grown up and become a woman.

EIGHT
A New High
(No Prescription
Necessary)

We arrived at our new destination on a Thursday and received an invitation to attend the Friday night party held weekly for officers and their wives. I wanted to spend that first weekend with Father, but learned he was away for two weeks. Although I was very disappointed initially, I decided my time could best be used in getting our family settled.

My joy and enthusiasm over our new home was somewhat overshadowed by the inevitable. Within a few weeks I would be out of the Dexedrines and a new source for the pills would have to be found. My weight was coming off with the help of the pills, but somehow I had to convince Bob that I must continue on them beyond my desired weight loss. Now feeling secure in my marriage, I didn't need the pills as an emotional crutch; rather, I wanted to keep the weight off permanently.

We arrived at the officers' party at 8:00 Friday evening. Upon entering the crowded, smoke-filled room, we nearly had to shout at each other to hear over the din of the party. Blending into my new surroundings was not easy. New faces . . . a new language . . . a new life style. Insecurities nagged at me again. Would I be accepted and liked, or would I experience rejection? Would Bob be well received and would the other officers see his worth?

Everyone was drinking cocktails, and in order to help us blend into the atmosphere, Bob went to the bar and ordered two drinks. Perhaps a drink would make it easier for me to handle the deluge of new faces and rapid conversation.

In the past I had the sense to stay away from alcohol because of the complication it might have caused with the Dexedrine. I often heard of the deadly results of mixing liquor and pills. I never particularly cared for the taste of liquor and I could get plenty of emotional kicks from the pills. But tonight I would make an exception and show our new circle of friends and acquaintances that I fit in perfectly with their life style.

The tension of the evening worsened, and a combination of off-color conversation and trivia forced me to take an additional drink, and then another. I was sure that as long as I held a drink in my hands I could be gracious to the officers and their wives and make a far more favorable impression. Different people kept putting a new drink in my hands, and I enjoyed the feeling of confidence alcohol gave me. It wasn't a

Dexedrine high, but a relaxing assurance that I could handle almost any pressure.

I tried to swing the conversations toward astrology. I felt that it might be a subject of interest to everyone, and it was my favorite topic. I knew that in the past I could attract a group of people and favorably impress them with my knowledge of the subject. It was a clever gimmick on my part to always be on top of a conversation and stay in control of things. I could be sure to impress people with my unusual knowledge of their personality and future, all charted by the stars and astrological signs.

Several of the officers were intrigued, and kept buying me drinks throughout the evening. Bob roamed the area, meeting fellow officers, feeling sure I could handle the new situation on my own. What a mistake, for I couldn't see the change coming over me.

I began to get silly and to laugh loudly. I interrupted conversations, and had trouble getting words out. I caught myself keeping my balance by leaning on officers. Worst of all, I never noticed the amused glances at me.

Bob came up from behind and put his arm around me.

"We'd better go," he said softly. I thought I saw him make an apologetic glance at one of the other officers and a new wave of guilt swept over me. Had my lack of self-control brought disfavor to Bob? Had I humiliated him, or worse, spoiled his chances of promotion?

The real agony of those thoughts would descend later; right now I was enjoying the sensation of a new high. This time it came from a chemical for which no prescription was necessary.

Bob helped me to the car and watched sadly as I plunked down on the car seat with a thud. I watched the world around me spin for a few seconds. At the very least I deserved a severe scolding, but Bob got into the car silently. I felt my guilt compound in his silence.

"Honey, I'm sorry," I said awkwardly. "It happened so fast. The drinks make me more relaxed with the new faces. I was afraid we wouldn't make a good impression if I was uptight. I guess I don't do anything in moderation, do I?"

"It's OK," he said reassuringly.

I leaned my head back on the car seat and closed my eyes. I had much to be grateful for and little need to have crutches in life. And yet there was a new wave of temptation overcoming me. I felt an unusual attraction to this new drug: alcohol.

The next morning I sat sipping coffee alone at the breakfast table. Bob had been called to work that morning and little Mark was still asleep. I never wanted to humiliate Bob again and yet I realized what a slave I was to anything that felt good. I had an overwhelming desire to experience pleasure from liquor again right away. I knew that it was just another crutch, but I didn't really care. I was also aware that it could drive a wedge between Bob and me.

Nevertheless, the pull within myself toward this new intrigue was almost supernatural. I seemed a marked target for the roaming demon of intoxication. Common sense did little to convince me that two intoxications—the liquor and the pills—would be deadly. As though I were a puppet pulled by strings, I prepared myself to dress and take a trip to the nearby liquor store. And as I began to leave an hour later, with Mark in my arms, I rationalized my behavior quite simply: if I drank often during the week, by Friday night's party I would be able to hold my liquor well and still make a favorable impression.

That week I approached my new project enthusiastically. I didn't share it with Bob, but kept a bottle of gin well hidden in a laundry basket. I gradually increased the quantity of liquor I consumed, so that by Friday I could have several drinks and not be affected. I started out the project with caution, concerned about the combination of pills and liquor, but at the end of the first day I didn't feel any adverse effects. Instead, I experienced a new kind of euphoria and pressure-free existence. Nothing bothered me, including the demands of the baby or the fears of starting over in a new city and not being accepted.

That Friday night I passed the test. I kept careful track of the number of drinks I took and knew well what my limit was because of the "test run" I had worked on during the week. I drank just enough to stay in control and be charming and interested in dull conversation. I had an unusual boldness and lost some fear of strangers. How typical of me to focus only on the positive effects of the new chemical and to disregard all the consequences. I would have to learn the hard way.

Father finally returned and we made plans to visit. I was on a natural high anticipating our time together. I felt on top of the world. But what if he and Bob didn't hit it off? I hardly noticed that every time a conflict entered my mind I reached for my bottle of vodka or gin and mixed a drink.

Father beamed at the sight of his grandson and received Bob warmly into the family. He gave Bob a bear-hug that said he approved of my choice. Father had a drink in his hand and he mixed a drink for Bob and me and several more for himself over a period of an hour. I silently looked back on the years of childhood and saw how alcohol must have divided our home. I made a mental note to myself never to allow it to get in the way of my home, then washed away any guilt feelings with another swallow of vodka and lemonade.

I saw approval in Father's eyes and I breathed a quiet sigh of relief. I was thankful for the Dexedrine, for it had enabled me to lose a good deal of weight. Now that I was taking one every two hours I could experience a pleasant high and loss of appetite without being hyper. Being reunited with Father and belonging to Bob Abrams brought me a warm feeling of security and love. Now my only anxiety was convincing Bob that I must stay on the pills and find a new supplier. That confrontation lay around the corner, but for now I would bask in the look of approval on Father's face, the contentment of the son in my lap, and the feeling of security I had with Bob's arm around my shoulder.

By the time my supply of Dexedrine was exhausted I hadn't lost the desired amount of weight. When I gave him a verbal promise that I would cut down on the pills and only drink socially, Bob found me another supply of Dexedrine. I dropped down to one Dexedrine every three hours, but decided to compensate for that by drinking more. However, I made sure Bob didn't see me drink other than occasionally with friends or at the officers' party. The added amounts of alcohol would act as the appetite depressant I needed to compensate for fewer Dexedrine.

The months rolled by quickly and I bathed in the luxury of being near my loved ones—Mark, Bob, and Father. Nevertheless, I began drinking earlier and earlier in the day and waited for the surge of renewed self-confidence that came with the alcohol. I saw my figure inch down to the desired hundred pounds and each day I liked myself more. What a con artist I was; however, my self-imposed guilt-trips were quickly washed away with a drink.

At first I only denied myself some luxuries and used money Bob gave me for the liquor. As my thirst grew I took some grocery money and bought fewer household items, keeping several bottles a week stored in secret places—underwear drawers, laundry baskets, and backs of cupboards. The game kept me alert; fortunately,

Bob never asked me to account for the money he gave me.

For the first time in years life was smooth. I should have known, however, that it was only the calm before the storm. I received a letter from Mother saying that she planned to fly out to visit us. I knew now my secret would come out in the open, for now my days would no longer be spent in solitude. The con-game was coming to an end. The best I could hope for was that Mother would keep Bob from discovering my drinking.

I had really missed Mother since our move to California. How unfortunate that now I looked upon her visit as a burden! It should have been a carefree time with loved ones, but I faced the visit with total apprehension. I continued to acquire a growing taste and desire for alcohol. Having learned of chemical dependency through Dexedrine, I should have exercised a greater caution with my newfound pastime of drinking. I even understood how paradoxical my situation was—my heart's desire was to make Bob and Mark happy, yet I continued on a slow road to self-destruction.

Mother's perception of my new fascination with alcohol was quick as usual. In less than a day she had figured out that I was drinking off and on throughout the day. Thus an argument with Mother ushered in almost every new day, and her nagging dragged out the hours endlessly. Even sneaking a drink of odorless vodka couldn't be kept a secret. My only relief was the afternoon walk she took with little Mark. While they were gone I generously mixed myself several drinks to prepare for the nagging when she returned. By the time Bob came home in the early evening, I was riddled with anxiety waiting for Mother to announce to Bob the fact that I spent a good part of each day drinking. In my somewhat twisted frame of mind, I felt Mother was plotting against me rather than making a desperate attempt to help her daughter.

For ten days she kept her silence about the drinking. I thought I was home free the day she prepared to leave. I breathed a sigh of relief, for Mother seemed quietly resigned to the abuse of the pills and alcohol. In reality, her concern over the situation boiled beneath the surface like a churning volcano whose inevitable fate was eruption.

Mother had gone to our guest room to gather some things together on her last evening. Bob sat with his feet up in the lounging chair, studying the evening paper. He was unaware of the cold war that had been going on for nearly two weeks in his home between Mother and me. Mark was playing contentedly at his feet.

Suddenly Mother appeared in front of Bob with a look that said she was ready for battle. It sent a chill through me, for it implied she had kept still long enough. I desperately shook my head at her, hoping she would keep our secret. It was too late.

"Bob, you've got to stop Sandy's excessive drinking. She drinks nearly all day, you know. It's bad enough that you allow her those pills. I see her sneak a drink a dozen times a day. I can't watch my daughter destroy herself, but I can't make her stop. Will *you*?" Mother's voice was stern but caring. She had planted herself firmly in front of Bob as he looked at her over the paper. In the few seconds of silence that followed Mother's words, I thought of a million more lies I could fabricate, but what was the use?

Bob set the paper down on his lap and removed his glasses. He had a puzzled on his face as he faced me. I realized that what hurt him the most was my lack of openness and honesty with him.

"Is it true?" Bob's words were soft but pointed. My own self-condemnation made me want to run out the door and just keep going, but I could never walk out on those that meant so much to me.

"I drink a little during the day," I said defensively. "Just a few drinks. It's under control."

"Tell him everything," Mother urged. "How you hide the bottles of vodka in the hamper or behind the spices in the kitchen."

"It helps depress my appetite and makes me feel generally better." The words came out haltingly as I tried to defend myself.

"But you're more than acceptable the way you are to Mark and me," Bob replied.

My mind raced through several long moments of silence. It seemed that my personality and desires fluctuated with the wind. A large part of me wanted to just stay at home and make my family happy, and yet there was a strong need within me to be socially acceptable and even be a successful business woman someday. My personality often changed, depending on my weight. When I was heavy, I was much more content to stay at home; when I was thin, I had tremendous energy and zest for life. I wanted people around and desired to be active. But I was never thoroughly happy with either role.

Yes, I was acceptable to Bob and Mark and I knew it. So why complicate my life? Was there some inner force that drove me to a self-destructive end? An inner force that even superseded the tremendous love I had for my family?

Mother sat down on the sofa and seemed relieved that she had spoken up. But now she felt awkward, having been responsible for some tension in the air.

"I can take a walk if you two want to talk," she said softly.

"No, Mother." I came and sat by her on the couch. "You did the right thing. You did it because you love me and it's OK. You hurt me to help me. But I'm not an alcoholic now and I can easily stop drinking. I can even cut out the pills, but that will take a little longer. Mother, I want you to fly home tonight as you planned, and in six months I'll come visit you. You'll see then, because I'll be off the pills and my drinking will be under control. Would you both trust me?"

I had said it convincingly. I was even impressed with my own sincerity.

"I want you to go home and not worry about me," I continued.

Mother nodded her approval, then looked to Bob for more reassurance.

"It will be all right," he said. "For whatever Sandy does wrong, she does a lot more right."

"If you love her, then be firm," Mother insisted. Bob shook his head and had a look that said he would do everything he could.

But how quickly and painlessly promises are broken. In the ensuing year in Oakland, very little changed. As long as I could get away with the drinking during the day, I just kept increasing the amount of alcohol daily. Bob continued to find a source of the Dexedrine for me as long as I kept them down to eight a day; I went along with that because I could compensate for a desired sixteen a day with increased quantities of alcohol. I continued to rationalize my actions by feeling that I must present the very best possible outward appearance for Bob. I would help him and earn him an early promotion. Having perfect outward appearance was becoming an obsession.

At the end of our stay in Oakland, Bob was offered a promising job as a stockbroker back in Minneapolis. It had been a good two years in Oakland. Any fear or insecurity had been easily washed away by my cop-out devices. Living near Father had been a dream come true. And I finally felt free from the chains of the past because of the tremendous lift I got from the chemicals.

But what a paradox, for I couldn't actually see what a prisoner to myself I was becoming.

NINE
No Room at the Top

I allowed myself the luxury of basking in our new life style in Minneapolis. I felt I had it made—I had just about everything a young wife and mother could want. My marriage was solid, and I enjoyed the security it offered. Yet there was still that compulsion to keep my weight down and be even more acceptable. Bob often reinforced my obsession with my outward appearance by giving me expensive new clothes. It was a subtle reminder that he wanted me to always look my best, which drove me to increased quantities of the pills to maintain a perfect weight.

Some months later, however, pressures at his new job forced Bob to be more detached from home. My own anxiety over that situation caused me to drink more heavily. Slowly I increased the quantities of both pills and alcohol and those subtle insecurities were washed away.

Mother continued to stand by in hopeless frustration watching me abuse these things. She was becoming more and more involved with God and religion. She began to urge me to let God help me, but her God was Jesus and Bob would never go along with any interest shown in this Gentile God.

The year Mark turned four I had a neighborhood birthday party for him. I planned for it for weeks—making elaborate decorations and preparing a cake that would impress the forty children we had invited. For several days I shopped for gifts that would delight him. It would be the highlight of his young life.

But the pressures of preparing for the party caused me to start drinking by 10:00 A.M. That morning the alcohol had an unusual effect on me. I'd experienced such a reaction occasionally when I took too many Dexedrine pills over a period of days. By 11:30 my head was spinning and I had just enough presence of mind to call Mother to help pull off the party.

Mark knew something was wrong. He had never seen me lose control from a drink, but by the time Mother arrived, I was face down on the kitchen table trying desperately not to pass out.

Mother helped me to my room, and as she did so I caught a glimpse of little Mark. Confusion and disappointment shrouded his face. His mother appeared too sick to pull off his big day. My mind was too muddled to try to make an explanation to him.

But Mother stepped in to pull off the party for me. I lay helpless in my room, drifting in and out of awareness, unsure if thoughts were dreams, fantasies, or reality. I heard the piercing ring of the doorbell several times, followed by the excited voices of little children.

I lost track of time. Every now and then the bedroom door would open and then close. Once I opened my eyes and looked right into the eyes of Mark who stood beside me. He looked sadly at me as he held two of his birthday presents. His eyes communicated deeply at that moment: love, sympathy, pity, and disappointment.

Then Mother appeared at the door and took Mark away. He turned back to look at me again and in that brief moment I saw clearly how my own lack of self-control and self-discipline finally touched the life of my son.

Mother came in shortly after that and found me sitting on the edge of the bed with my head in my hands. She sat beside me for several moments, wanting to comfort me but finding it difficult to show love after my behavior that day. Finally she put her arm around my shoulder.

"Let someone help you," she said quietly. "You can't do it on your own."

"Who, Mother?"

"Jesus, And maybe the pastor at my church."

"Why would Jesus want to help me? Since marrying Bob I finally feel Jewish, and Jews don't believe in Jesus."

"Jesus changes lives. He gives new life."

It sounded simplistic. "It's just not for me," I insisted softly. "Not now anyway. I'm willing to get help because I see how I hurt my son today. But I'll get help some other way. You can pray for me all you want, but don't push Jesus on me."

"Without God you'll only make vain attempts and empty promises to quit destroying yourself," Mother continued.

"Once before I told you I'd quit drinking," I said. "I didn't mean it, I guess. But I'm telling you again. I am going to quit for the sake of my family. I'll do it on my own; I'm a strong person. I may even pray to God, but not Jesus right now. Try to understand. Bringing Jesus into this house would only complicate matters."

I kept my promise to Mother for less than six hours before that inner compulsion drove me right back to my bottle of vodka. Along with that compulsion was the nagging guilt and depression that had to be soothed. That kind of guilt and depression could easily drive me back to the comforts of food. It was a vicious circle.

Some weeks later I learned that I was pregnant again. As with the last pregnancy, I determined to give the baby a fair start in life. The Dexedrine had to go—again a sacrifice on my part only because I didn't want my child to have to directly pay for my problems. But my alcohol consumption could not be cut back. Liquor would make withdrawal from the pills more bearable and it would help check my appetite to a certain degree. As a matter of fact, the drinking would have to increase in order to compensate.

This time alcohol eased my withdrawal from the Dexedrine. Nevertheless, breaking the chains of such a bondage required support and encouragement. Bob gave that to me, but I sensed that next time he wouldn't be quite so understanding or tolerant when I would ask to go back on the pills. But the four-day withdrawal period was cut in half and the pain eased with heavy drinking throughout the ordeal.

Our second son, Ross, was born some time later. Again came the bitter with the sweet: I had a beautiful new baby that resembled his father very much; but I'd gained over sixty pounds. Though there was little evidence to support my fear, I even imagined I could lose Bob now that I had outgrown all the new clothes he had bought me earlier.

And now I faced an additional agony. In order to nurse the baby, I had to go off the alcohol also. For the sake of my son I had to purge myself. And without both the pills and the liquor, even more weight gain was inevitable. For the next six months I would have to draw on some kind of inner strength to help me see my son as far more important than any habit.

I felt that a mother's love for her child would make this awesome task possible. Indeed, that was a strong motivating force; but I realized my need to draw upon something or someone stronger than I was. Call it God or a higher power—a source of strength that I presently knew nothing about. Since I did not know where to find that Source, I fought the battle to free myself from these bondages. Even with some support fom Bob and Mother, initially it seemed to be an obstacle course. Yet it turned out to be one of the more rewarding times of my life: I was actually able to give up a sizable part of me for someone else.

But six months later I'd gained even more weight. I desperately tried to think of a new angle to hit Bob with, in hopes that he would find me another supply of the Dexedrine. I'd lost track of the times I'd said, "Just help me one more time. When I lose the weight, I'll quit." A widening communication gap between Bob and me made me frantic to resume my drinking and Dexedrine. Not only would it result in weight loss, it would also ease the nagging ache brought on by Bob's increased silence at home.

But once again Bob agreed to help me get the pills until I could lose the desired weight. Again I promised him that for the sake of the family I would quit taking them when the pounds came off. And I began to go to extra lengths to convince Bob that he and the boys were my whole life. We began to have a Friday evening Sabbath service in our home. I prayed over the candles and fixed an appropriate meal.

I made a happy family occasion out of the Jewish New Year, Passover, Yom Kippur, and Hanukkah. We even kept a kosher home during Passover.

I made an extra effort to encourage Bob at his job, though he shared little about that area of his life. I bought him little gifts, or frequently fixed his favorite meal.

A pleasant by-product of my attempt to have a nice Jewish home was a restored and improved relationship with Leonard, my stepfather. Our mutual interest in Judaism would be the cement that could draw us closer. I could at least please him by sharing his faith, even if I could not please Mother.

I set aside each Sunday for a family occasion. In the future my children would always be able to look forward to birthdays and other special occasions without the interference of my chemical dependencies. It took careful coordinating to manage motherly details properly while still drinking and taking pills to excess. Though I was a slave to my own needs, still the lives of my family were of utmost importance to me. With almost superhuman discipline, I managed to fulfill my own needs, but not at their expense.

And so, because of my continued indulgence with the Dexedrine and the alcohol, the excess weight was lost. Also because of these stimulants, my personality resorted back to its outgoing, confident style. I was happy to entertain company for Bob and be as socially active as possible. I was sure that not only by outward appearance were our marriage and home secure; I was convinced within myself that all was well and that Bob's increasing silence stemmed from business pressures. The fact was, I saw only what I wanted to see; in reality, Bob was slowly drifting away from me.

Bob was being promoted quickly within the company and we headed toward an upper-class life style. My responsibilities increased along with his. By the time the boys were three and seven I found I had to entertain company for Bob frequently. The pressure of doing the very best possible job drove me to more excessive drinking. I drank to keep calm and to give myself self-confidence as I entertained. I continued steadily on with the Dexedrine as added insurance that I wouldn't gain weight and lose favor in the eyes of Bob and his business associates. In spite of my broken promises, Bob kept finding me an adequate supply of the pills. He was unaware, however, that I was again back to a dozen or more pills, accompanied by at least a quart of alcohol, a day.

At first we experienced accelerating spending in our new economic status. I went on buying binges, crowding out nearly every closet in our home with my luxurious wardrobe. I bought designer fashions and had a seventy-five-dollar-a month bill at the finest beauty salon in Minneapolis. I bought the boys hundreds of toys. Bob hired a girl to live in with us and help me with the house and the children. This conveniently allowed me more time to go on the shopping sprees and to have free afternoons to lounge at the country club pool.

I opened up a private charge account at a

nearby liquor store and consistently ran up a several-hundred-dollar bill which I wanted to keep secret from Bob. He was still unaware of my excessive drinking, and since I functioned well in the role of wife and mother, he never became overly suspicious. Besides, he was spending increased time away from home.

But the luxury living was short-lived. Soon Bob began to come home with a deep look of concern on his face. Though he shared no details, something was happening that was deepening the lines on his face and causing him to withdraw further. As I opened a closet to show him my latest purchase, his anxiety finally spilled over and the flood waters broke through the proverbial dam.

"That's it, Sandy," he said nervously. "No more outfits. This is the last."

"What's wrong?"

"I haven't wanted to tell you. Business is bad. The company is being shaken up. It's serious."

"Why didn't you tell me sooner?"

"Because you don't handle bad news very well. My salary was cut this month. It will be until business picks up. For the next few months you've got to cut out all this spending, OK? Don't buy anything unless it's absolutely necessary."

But the spending sprees had become a bondage to me just like the Dexedrine and the alcohol. I felt compelled to keep on buying new things. I opened up several charge accounts that

I planned to keep from Bob and tried to push out of my mind the fact that someday the accounts would have to be paid.

Then I began to dread each day's mail, for it brought that inevitable bill for my excessive buying. I kept them all from Bob, but I began to dread the fact that the creditors would call him as the bills became more and more overdue! Soon my clothes, liquor, and beauty salon bills totaled more than $4,000. The worst of it was that it didn't stop me from buying more. As a matter of fact, I soothed my conscience by running out and spending more money.

But when Bob began receiving calls from the creditors I knew I had to find help. I promised him I would somehow pay off the bills, and it occurred to me that my stepdad, Leonard, could be of help. I had asked him for very little in life; perhaps that was a mistake. When I explained my situation to him, he reacted with honest compassion and concern. Perhaps he saw this as an opportunity to show me the love I had always wanted from him. In any case, I deeply regretted that I hadn't come to him earlier in life.

The only catch to his loaning me $4,000 was that I had to close every account I had! I paid the bills, closed all accounts, and had financial freedom for three days. I then went out and opened five new accounts that week and three the next. Within two weeks I was right back in the same dilemma, with more creditors hounding me. I never did anything in moderation.

Bob began coming home later and later at

night. Communication between us worsened, but I chose to blame it on pressures at the office. He was caught up in that problem, and he admittedly didn't want to worry me with it. I convinced myself that that was the sole reason for his silence.

But amid these pressures, I received word of my third pregnancy. It meant, of course, going off the Dexedrine again and the inevitable weight gain. Perhaps the new baby would draw us closer; maybe it would get his mind off the things that were causing him to withdraw.

Once again I faced the struggle of coming off the pills. Again alcohol cushioned the blow, but not without two agonizing days of breaking the chains of addiction. Along with that, I had to face the prospect of nine more months of tremendous weight gain.

I was overjoyed to have a baby girl, but I quickly realized that Stephanie was going to receive all of Bob's attention. I found real jealousy creeping into my attitude toward Bob and my little girl, and I became very angry at my tremendous weight gain. As I stared at my unattractive figure in the mirror I felt sure that my obesity was the reason Bob showered most of his love on Stephanie. In desperation I went back on the pills and increased my drinking even more.

Bob rehired Ginny, the live-in girl, who helped me with the children. Because of her help, I again had the freedom to spend afternoons away from home, usually around the pool at the country club. I found satisfaction in meeting new people. Many of them were men, and as I lost the weight, I found some satisfaction and approval in their admiring glances.

One late afternoon in August I arrived home from the pool to find the house in confusion. Ginny was packing her suitcase in her room. The boys seemed upset, but they weren't crying or making a fuss. By the confused look on their faces I knew something was definitely wrong.

I questioned Ginny as she took her things out of the dresser drawer and packed them into her suitcase.

"Where are you going? I haven't dismissed you, Ginny."

"Mr. Abrams did this afternoon. He said I should go because he wouldn't be paying me anymore, Mrs. Abrams."

"Why didn't he consult me? What's going on?"

"He said he left you a note in the bedroom that would explain things. He paid me for this week, Mrs. Abrams, but said I should leave today. If that's all right with you, I'll be going now."

I didn't answer Ginny but went to the bedroom and looked on the dresser. Next to my picture was Bob's wedding ring and a note. It was short and simple: "Sandy, I've left you. Here's $200 for now and I'll call in a few days to see what you need. I'm sorry. Bob."

It had to be a joke. Surely it couldn't be for real.

"Goodbye, Mrs. Abrams." It was Ginny

calling as she waited at the front door for her ride. I went to the top of the stairs and called down to her. She was already out the door, and I was alone in the house with the children.

I called Mother frantically and asked her to come over. This couldn't be happening to me, could it? Couldn't I awaken and find I was dreaming? Was Bob playing a cruel trick on me? Was he just trying to scare me out of my self-centered existence? I'd try to be better—just give me another chance, someone!

I retrieved a bottle of vodka from a closet and searched every room in the house. Maybe this was just a game of cat and mouse or hide and seek. But every room echoed emptily, and even the boys' voices sounded strangely muffled and distant. I carried the bottle of vodka back to the bedroom and changed clothes. Then I flew down the stairs, passing Mother as she entered the front door. Without explanation, I got into the car while Mother looked on in confusion.

"Mother, don't worry. I'm going for a ride to get my head back together." I guzzled the vodka as I sat behind the wheel in the driveway. Barely noticing Mother's scared expression, I screeched the tires and pulled out of the driveway down the narrow suburban street. I caught a glimpse of Mother through the rear-view mirror as she stood frozen to the ground, watching me speed away.

As I drove onto the freeway I gave serious thought to simply driving the car into the highway divider. But something kept me from following the suicidal impulse. Instead, I increased my speed to nearly ninety miles an hour. I darted in and out of lanes, obsessed with the idea of just letting go of the wheel and allowing fate to take control of the outcome.

Other motorists looked at me in disbelief as I seemed to be heading for an unknown destination, first in one lane and then another. One hand was on the wheel and the other cradled the only comfort I was acquainted with—my bottle of vodka.

It occurred to me that maybe Bob had come home by now. Surely he just wanted to frighten me, and since he'd succeeded at that, the game was over. I sped back to the house, wondering where on earth all the police cars were that frequented our area. Although I had greatly exceeded the speed limit, there wasn't a single patrol car in sight.

I rounded the corner to the house and looked hopefully in the driveway. Bob's car wasn't there, but maybe it was now in the garage. The brakes screeched again as I stopped in the driveway. Leaving the motor running, I grabbed the vodka and rushed into the house again.

My panic-stricken mother tried to stop me for some explanations, but I pushed her away and searched the house for Bob. Feeling ghostly white, I came into the kitchen where Mother sat with her hand on the telephone.

"What are you doing, Mother?"

"Calling the hospital to get you admitted." Her voice sounded resigned to my behavior. I took the receiver from her hand and slammed it down.

"I'm all right, Mother. Bob has left, but I'll be OK. I just need to be alone and think for a while. Take the children, will you? Just for a week or so, please?"

"You'll just drink yourself into a stupor. I don't trust you alone in the house." Mother reached for the phone again.

"No! Bob will be back and I'll be all right. I just need a few days without the kids around so I can collect my thoughts. Please, Mother. I'll call you every day to let you know I'm OK."

"Sandy, you must let someone help you. Perhaps a doctor could prescribe something to help calm you down. Or perhaps my pastor can help you. He can help you find comfort through the love of Jesus, Sandy."

"No, Mother, I don't want to hear about that Jesus stuff. Not now anyway. I'm already too confused. I just want to be alone, OK? I'll call you tonight, but please take the children with you."

I escaped to my bedroom and to the generous supply of vodka hidden in my dresser drawer. After locking the bedroom door, I went straight to the drawer and took out two bottles. For the next three days I drank myself into a state of semiconsciousness. Mother called several times a day but I let the phone ring annoyingly, not answering. I lost track of the time but was eventually awakened by a knocking at the bedroom door. It was Mother and my stepdad, Leonard, who had become alarmed at the lack of response to their phone calls. The knocking grew louder and louder and it felt as though they were hitting my head rather than the door. To ease the annoyance I let them in. They badgered me about ruining my life and their life and my children's lives. When would I get some help? I covered my ears with my hands and sat on the edge of the bed. I was too weak to fight back or to reply in any way.

I stayed close to home in the coming weeks, perhaps expecting Bob to come through the door. But confirmation of our separation occurred when he finally called one rainy Sunday afternoon. News like this always hits on such days. Divorce proceedings had started and that official death sentence to my marriage drove me to deeper despair.

Added to my depression was the realization that without Bob I would have to find my own Dexedrine source. Both the inconvenience and expense of that idea were hardly appealing. I had only a two-day supply of the pills left, and I was sure I wouldn't have the ability to cope with life right now without them.

I got up from the bed to reach for a bottle of vodka on the dresser, but caught a glimpse of myself in the mirror. I stopped for a closer look. I was thirty going on fifty. My body felt like a spinning top that had just had its last turn. My eyes were sunken and lifeless. My nerves were shattered and my emotions could only function with a chemical telling them what to do. My children suffered the most from my behavior, but maybe there was still time to make it up to them.

I set the bottle of vodka down and reached for the phone by the bed. With shaking hands I dialed Mother's number. Would she ever answer?

"Hello, Mother." My voice was shaking. "Would you come and get me? Make the arrangements for me, would you? Some hospital where I can dry out and get my head together. Today, please."

I hung up, closed my eyes, and leaned back on the pillow. For several moments I experienced a totally new feeling. It was called letting go.

TEN
Stop the World, I Want to Get Off!

As I entered the Psychiatric Ward, I was frightened and apprehensive. How long would I be separated from Mark, Ross, and Stephanie? What kind of physical discomfort would I go through to dry out and get off the pills? Worst of all, what assurance did I have that I would stay off of them? My track record was already poor.

I was escorted to my room—sterile white with barren walls. The room seemed like a reflection of me—empty, cold, and lacking expression.

I was asked to give up everything in my possession including my wedding ring. Since it was the only memory I really had of Bob, it seemed like a shred of security. I just couldn't give it to the hospital—even temporarily. Fortunately, the nurse accepted my refusal understandingly and then left me to unpack my suitcase and familiarize myself with things. I sank onto the bed wishing that someone could offer me peace, happiness, and fulfillment—at no sacrifice to me; on sort of a buy-now-and-never-pay basis.

At some point in the confusion of checking in, I had heard someone say I'd be here six weeks. That was the usual time needed for drying out, group therapy, private counseling, and drug therapy. Now I began to wonder, was this all an exercise in futility? No! I would not be defeated before I started. I would program myself for success—not failure. I would envision myself six weeks from now as a transformed person! It couldn't be worse than a six-week diet. However, the diet must become a new life style and not just a crash course. It occurred to me to try prayer, for Mother had been sharing the results of prayer in her life. Could I swallow my pride and stubbornness and reach out to God? Not yet.

It had been several hours since my last shot of alcohol and my last Dexedrine, and now the shock that I was actually making the break set in. It was one thing to admit I'd given up and allow myself to be checked into the hospital. It was something else to enter the Psych Ward and to sit on the edge of a bed that was equipped to strap me in. The antiseptic smell of the hospital was apparent even in the Psych Ward. Although patients on this floor were allowed to dress in street clothes, I couldn't forget the fact that I was surrounded by desperate people. Was I so desperate? Maybe I'd made a drastic mistake.

Maybe I should go home and simply moderate my use of chemicals. Since there were no bars or padded cells, I could have walked out.

I looked out the window at the bustle of traffic below. The leaves would be off the trees before I completed the hospital program. Somehow waiting for a season to change seemed like forever. A week or two I could handle, but how could I endure six weeks of self-inflicted torture?

I pushed a button for the nurse to come to my room. Within seconds the door swung open and the nurse cheerfully asked what she could do for me. Her reassuring look helped calm the quaking fears I'd had since checking in.

"I'm getting sick, I think," I struggled to explain. "I don't know if I can take it—you know—I need something in place of the pills or booze."

"Yes, we're preparing something for you," she assured me. "We're going to give you some sedatives to help you get through withdrawal. It should take care of those symptoms for you."

I'd never heard of such a thing, but that relieved my mind to some extent. Each time I had faced these symptoms—whether strong or mild—I had vowed that I would never go through withdrawal again. But if there was a painless way to withdraw, why hadn't someone thought of it sooner?

The nurse disappeared, then returned a few moments later to give me an injection. I stared at the ceiling, lost in thought, barely noticing as she gave me the needle. Moments later, I experienced a pleasant euphoria that felt more like an escape from life than a physical sensation.

For the next ten days I seldom left my bed and enjoyed having some room service. Although the hospital staff encouraged activity among the patients, I was incapable, physically and emotionally, of doing anything. During the crisis period of withdrawal I received hypos and sedatives constantly. Despite my drugged state I kept anticipating the usual pain and discomfort, and I couldn't understand the delayed reaction. I was sure the symptoms would begin momentarily; yet, the hours passed with only the most minor discomfort. Other people could get away with this, I thought, but Sandy Abrams always paid heavily for everything. For a brief moment I wondered whether my mother's prayers had helped to make things easier this time. I was too drugged to think clearly, but I felt I wanted to thank someone for making phase one of this project bearable.

Overriding any physical suffering I endured was the severity of my loneliness. Fortunately, I was always too sleepy to realize that I could have dressed and walked out on the whole absurd scheme at almost any time.

On the tenth day, room service ended and I was asked to comply with the general rules of the floor. That meant group therapy twice a day for a total of six hours, plus recreational therapy. Now I had to leave the security of my small private room and go socialize; or worse yet, get into discussions that might uproot very personal problems. These were problems I really didn't want to share with anyone, let alone strangers who apeared to be more disturbed than I. How could I relate to the woman in the room next to me who was sure she was being poisoned by the hospital staff? I may have been chemically dependent, but I wasn't suffering from a mental illness and I didn't want to fraternize with such people. Private therapy in the confines of my room seemed more acceptable. But if I cooperated with the rules, Mark and Ross could come and see me three times a week. With that incentive I decided to participate, though half-heartedly.

I finally felt safe and cared for in the hospital, but that only encouraged me to slow down my progress. Thoughts of returning to the jungle outside frightened me and I was sure I could never fend for myself without Bob's protection. I felt so utterly alone, even with frequent visits from Mother, Leonard, and the children. Mother left me a Bible and encouraged me to read it, but I didn't know where to begin. Instead I decided to talk to God. I was so lonely and hungry for a good dialog that it didn't matter to me whether I was addressing the Jewish God or the Gentile God. All I knew was that I felt some peace after I prayed, and that maybe I'd been heard. But I began to get hung up on the mechanics of prayer—should I close my eyes or kneel? How should I really address myself to God—if indeed there is one? Should I sound eloquent or super-spiritual, or just be Sandy? Finally, instead of speaking to God, I wrote my prayers on paper and experienced some healing through getting my thoughts out in this form. I wanted to believe that somebody really cared enough to listen to me. But what if God was just a figment of my imagination?

I brought the written prayers to group therapy and hesitantly shared them. The other members said that I had resorted to cop-outs. They felt I should put my trust in myself or humanity or medicine, but not in some ethereal kill-joy who didn't want me to have any fun in life. At that point I couldn't deal with any rejection, so I played along and dumped the idea of prayer, written or spoken. God would have to nudge me harder if he really was out there.

After that difficult session I slowly walked back to my room. But my pace quickened as I heard my telephone ringing. I eagerly picked up the telephone, expecting Mother's voice.

"Hello, Sandy? Is that you?"

"Yes . . . yes. Is that you, Bob?" my voice became more enthusiastic as I recognized his voice. I hadn't heard from Bob since the day he had walked out of my life weeks before.

"Sandy, listen. I don't have much time to talk, but I really need your help." I wanted to jump in fervently and convince him that I would do *anything* for him, but he interrupted my rapid train of thought.

"I've got to sell the house, Sandy. My lawyer will be up to see you tomorrow so that you can sign the papers. You will sign them, won't you?"

Panic tore through me. How could I give up the house? It was the only bit of security I had left. How could Bob turn his family out in-to the street homeless?

"Bob . . . no. I can't let you sell the house. Couldn't you just come home? Bob, I'm off all that stuff now. The program here, well, it's really helping me. I think we could . . ."

His impatient voice interrupted again. I was jarred by his brusque manner and his lack of concern for me.

"No. I'm not coming home, but I've run into some financial problems and I need the money for the house. Sandy, you want child support, don't you? If you don't sign those papers tomorrow I'll leave the state and you won't get that support. Don't make me do it, OK? Just sign the papers."

Bob's businesslike voice convinced me of the finality of his decision to leave me. My silent, unspoken hope that Bob might yet return had been crushed.

"Don't make it rough on me, Sandy. If you do, I'll make it worse on you."

"Bob, I can't think right now. Why did you hit me with this now? Couldn't you have waited?" No response. "Couldn't you call me back?"

"My lawyer will be there at 3:00 tomorrow. Just remember what I said." Click. No good-byes. Just like that, without remorse, Bob had pronounced dead any possibility of our reuniting.

For several minutes I sat holding the receiver. More shattered dreams, plus fears of house-hunting, were not what I needed to speed my recovery! But then, who cared about recovery? What was the use? Maybe it would simplify things if I just didn't recover.

I was allowed to have a razor at the hospital since I was being treated for addictions and not depression. As the phone receiver slid out of my hand and onto the floor, I walked in a daze to the bathroom. Slowly I removed the blade from the razor and stared blankly into the mirror. How could I go on messing up people's lives and causing sadness and disappointment? Would anyone ever love me again? Did I even deserve to be loved? Probably not. And what was the use of loving if I would end up losing that love anyway? It would be better if I never took those risks and felt that pain again. And yet, without some feeling of belonging, there was no point to life; so why continue?

I put the razor to my wrist and pressed into the flesh. At the same moment I let out a scream which must have been heard on the entire floor. Within seconds two nurses were restraining me and treating the wound. I continued to scream and wrestled until more help arrived. I shouted inarticulate obscenities and kicked with the strength of a mule. Couldn't anyone understand the injustices I'd experienced in my thirty years?

I was carried to the bed and felt the familiar needle in my arm, knowing that tranquility would soon follow. But before I felt the effects of the sedative, those awful straps on the bed came around my arms and legs and pinned me down. I shouted in protest and fought hard, causing the straps to chafe my skin. Tears ran down my face and I longed to be comforted. Then drowsiness overcame me. My thinking became jumbled and I heard my door close as the nurses left me to my dream world. I couldn't fight off the effect of the drug, so I relaxed into a deep, artificial sleep.

At 4:00 A.M. I awakened, waiting for a glimpse of morning light and release from the straps.

Around 6:00 A.M. I saw the dawn breaking and heard the rustle of footsteps in the hall. Shortly afterward a nurse came in but wouldn't release me until the doctor could see me later that morning. That meant probably three more hours of lying helpless in discomfort and humiliation.

After this incident, my recovery was slow, complicated by my lack of desire to return to the world. A recreational therapy program helped me, and each day I created craft items that brought some degree of accomplishment and healing. I would learn that my recreational therapy bill alone would be over $500, but it was well worth it.

After ten weeks I returned home with a stern warning from the doctor never to drink again. Damage to my liver was already severe and I knew that continued alcohol use could result in serious injury and possibly death. But how was I to cope with solving these problems: finding a new home, a job, and a baby-sitter for the children? Fear of the unknown was always my biggest stumbling block, and now there were so many unknown factors in my life that it read like a final exam.

As I returned home that morning I heard the phone ringing as I struggled to open the door. It was Bob's lawyer, wasting no time informing me of realities. I had to be out of the house in thirty days. The $7,000 hospital bill was my responsibility. Bob's financial problems wouldn't allow him to help much with the support of the children. I was told I'd better find a good job immediately.

In less than twenty-four hours I would reach for a bottle of vodka and start the whole pattern all over again. It was the only way I could cope with the pressures of life.

ELEVEN
Somebody Love Me!

We moved to a rented home and I found a job as a receptionist in a health club. I continued to drink heavily, but couldn't face the hassle of finding more pills, so I never went back on them. My self-image tumbled nearly out of sight. I felt I was a failure to my children and myself for not staying dry. I really was not worthy of anyone's love, and yet I needed it so badly.

I watched as Mark, now twelve years old, began to withdraw from his friends and choose me as his only companion. He confided in me his embarrassment in having divorced parents. I watched his outgoing, confident personality wither away, as his life became shrouded with uncertainty.

Ross' insecurities became pronounced in a different way. One morning about 1:00 A.M. I was shaken by screams from his room. I was still up, drinking as usual. I came to the foot of the stairs just as Ross appeared at the door of his room. He looked hysterical and acted as if he had just looked death in the face. He was not really awake and yet not asleep. His face was red and he glared at me with the look of a wild man. He screamed again and uttered words I couldn't understand, then dashed down the stairs. Pushing me aside with the strength of an adult, he darted into the street.

As he ran down the street he continued to scream, and one by one lights of our neighbors' houses came on and everyone looked out to see what was happening outside.

I chased after Ross. My heart was racing with fear and bewilderment, for I was sure Ross had completely lost his mind through the confusion of recent months.

It seemed as though Ross was controlled by a spirit. He was impossible to catch or to subdue, and he finally collapsed on the lawn of a home blocks away. When I reached him he was gasping for air, face down in the grass. His body was trembling and wet with perspiration on this chilly evening. I screamed for help and more lights went on in neighboring homes as confused, sleepy neighbors peered out into the darkness.

Moments later I heard the sirens of the rescue squad. Strangers gathered around the confused scene and tried to comfort me as my seven-year-old son lay on the ground.

I looked up into the pitch-black sky. How I wanted to call on God to intervene in the situation. Why did I feel so separated from God and so unworthy of his love?

Ross was given oxygen and his trembling, heavy breathing subsided. Just as mysteriously as he had entered into the seizure, he came out of it and looked up at me in confusion.

"I've had a nightmare, Mom," he said, unaware of all that had just taken place. He didn't even see the dozen people standing over him or sense the cool night air. He just closed his eyes and fell deeply asleep while being carried home.

The horror of that night repeated itself at least twice a week. I stayed up most nights waiting for the nightmare, seizure, or whatever it was, to start all over. Anticipating it drove me to heavier drinking. I had various friends take turns staying with me, hoping that two could restrain Ross if I couldn't alone. I finally had to take him out of school and put him under the care of a psychologist. Soon the problem subsided.

I began my workday at 6:30 A.M., at first working only on men's days at the health club. If I wanted to, I could work until 10:00 P.M. to earn additional money, but this meant juggling the children around all day—from school and day-care center to baby-sitters. The resulting guilt gnawed at me nonstop; and yet, to support my family, I had no choice but to work.

Another complicating problem was my unfulfilled need to drink on the job. I had my last drink in my car before entering the health club at 6:30 A.M. Somehow, it had to last until lunchtime; but the anticipation of my need caused me hours of desperate clock-watching. Even if I took an early drinking lunch to get some relief, I'd have to come back in the afternoon and watch the clock inch forward until dinnertime.

It was convenient for me to be working on men's days, for if I played my cards right I could have a luncheon date with a different club member each day. It fulfilled several needs—the need for acceptance, approval, and even love; and the need to have drinks provided at noon.

At every lunch date I ordered six Black Russians, because I knew of their high alcohol content. The six drinks could get me through most of the afternoon, and I held my liquor well enough so that nobody knew I was drinking.

I was so lonely I readily accepted all the attention I received at the club. The friendships, dates, and romances eased the painful memories of Bob. When I didn't have a diversion, I was nearly obsessed with the life Bob and I had shared, just as I had been obsessed at one time with memories of Father. Keeping Bob off my mind was very difficult since Ross was a mirror image of his father. Consequently, the children saw a variety of men frequent our home at all hours. The encounters with men took me away from my children even more and heaped coals upon my ever-present guilt.

I continued to chart my life by horoscopes. They forewarned me of bad days and predicted too accurately the good. They gave me insights into the men I was seeing and I usually dropped men that didn't score high enough on the astrology chart. I "guarded" my children through the horoscope and even kept them home when the predictions for the day could have harmed them. Before making any decision I consulted my astrology books Now, as I look back, I see how astrology was a gimmick in my life that opened the door for Satan to enter and take control.

As with everything else, I played the game of romantic musical chairs with utmost enthusiam. I never did anything half-heartedly. I practically ushered one man out the back door and another in the front. It was all a desperate attempt to find love and acceptance and to escape from my loneliness.

TWELVE
From Crisis to Christ

Steve was different from most of the men I had been seeing. He liked the children and included them in some of the things we did together. When he suggested taking us all on a weekend camping trip, we were delighted. We needed a family event to draw us closer.

We acquired a new addition to our family shortly before the camping trip: Woodstock, the family dog. Having Woodstock was very therapeutic for Mark, as they were constant companions. Mark's personality and confidence came back somewhat, because now he had a good friend who would never leave him.

The first night of our camping excursion was uneventful. We asked Mark to get up early the next morning and gather firewood for us to use to cook breakfast. At 6:00 A.M., Mark carefully tucked the hatchet under his belt and left the camp site with Woodstock. As I heard them go off into the woods, I was confident that Mark's Boy Scout training would keep them safe.

An hour later I got up, somewhat concerned that Mark hadn't returned. At 8:00 A.M. he was still gone and I felt sure something was wrong. Steve went out searching the area for Mark and Woodstock as I waited back at the camp site. Shortly after 9:00 A.M., Steve and two other campers came back without a clue. I grabbed a bottle of vodka and took Steve's car into town to find the police, but to my dismay I learned that a person had to be missing for ten hours before the police would begin a search. Ten hours! How could I endure the added hours of wondering and worry?

When I got back to the campground I learned that Steve had organized a number of campers to go out and continue the search. I took a full bottle of vodka with me and sat on a tree stump that overlooked a small river. It seemed I just couldn't escape this kind of frazzled life style. I began to cry softly and looked up through an empty space between trees to a pale blue sky. What assurance did I have that there was a God who could hear me if I did ask him for help?

Just then, a voice interrupted my thoughts. "May I give you this? It helped me through an ordeal. As a matter of fact, it helps me every day now."

I looked over my shoulder and saw one of the other women from the camp site standing over my shoulder, holding a Bible. Her comforting voice continued.

"You know, it's in times like these that God gives us strength. You will find words of comfort in this Bible," she said as she handed it to me.

"Sure. I guess it can't hurt," I replied, "but I don't know where to read."

"Well, you could start with the Psalms. The psalm-writer experienced tragedies and persecution, but God always delivered him. Maybe if you don't feel like reading, I could just sit here and read to you."

She took a few steps forward. "I'm not sure I believe in God," I replied apathetically. "He's awfully silent when I try to talk to him. Guess I need a sign or something that he exists."

"Then I'm going to pray today that you feel his very special presence," the stranger replied. "Do you know that there are several other campers who are praying for you and your son? We're going to pray for your boy, but also that God reveals himself to you through this ordeal. Do you believe God can do that?"

I gave a half-hearted nod that indicated skepticism, then turned away to stare blankly at the river again. I had gone to a Jewish funeral once where they read the twenty-third psalm. Maybe I could read that to start. I began to read, balancing the Bible in one hand and a bottle of vodka in the other.

But how could I step out in blind faith and

99

talk to what seemed to be an illusion in the sky? Should I bargain with God over Mark? I could give God my life if Mark was delivered safely. To whom should I address my petition? Should I direct it to God or Jesus? If it were true that they were one, as Mother said, I needn't worry about that. Couldn't God give me a sign to help me believe?

I looked up from the Bible to see one of Mark's tennis shoes float by me. I stared at it in horror as it bobbed up and down around the rocks, for it seemed to be God's way of showing me Mark's fate. This couldn't be!

I was ghostly white as I came back to the tent with the Bible in one hand and the vodka in the other. Campers looked at me with curiosity and compassion, and several came over to comfort and encourage me.

Ten hours passed and finally the police entered the search. They expressed concern that Woodstock had not returned, indicating that perhaps Mark was hurt and the dog wouldn't leave him. Other campers offered opinions and comments that did little to ease my anxiety. But whenever I opened the Bible I felt less agitated. However, I gave little credit to the woman's prayers for my deepened composure.

At eight that evening a helicopter was called into the search. The pilot kept us informed of his progress by relaying messages over his radio to a police officer. As I kept my vigil I decided that if there was a God, I wanted to put him to the test. I whispered, "Dear God, if you really exist, help them to find Mark before dark.

Don't make him spend the night alone, God. Bring him home by nine o'clock. God, if you bail me out of this and protect Mark, I promise I'll believe in you. Please, God.''

I went back to my tree stump to sit, think, and talk to God some more. It was growing dark and I constantly glanced at my watch. Why should God do me a favor? What had I ever done for him? Maybe a loving God wouldn't keep score. That was my only hope.

Suddenly a voice spoke from behind me. "Mrs. Abrams . . ." I turned and saw the police officer in charge. He had a huge grin on his face.

"Your son has been spotted. He's all right. The dog is OK, too."

I dropped the bottle of vodka and put my face in my hands. "Thank you, God," I whispered quietly.

"Your son is very clever," the police officer continued. "He took that hatchet and cut a bundle of logs, then climbed on top of an abandoned cabin. He spelled out S.O.S. with those logs, and that's how our 'copter spotted him. We'll have him here in a few minutes."

Moments later the helicopter touched down and Mark and Woodstock emerged, bug-bitten, scratched, but full of excitement about the day. Mark recounted the story for me . . . how he and Woodstock ran from what he thought was a bear, jumped into the river to escape, and then got turned around. The campers all breathed a sigh of relief and I caught a glimpse of the woman who had given me the Bible. I wanted to run up to her and tell her what had happened to me that day—how I had felt God's presence and peace—but Mark wouldn't stop talking long enough for me to break away.

I thanked God for the miracle of the day. My search to know God, or Jesus, had officially begun.

THIRTEEN
A Bridge over Troubled Waters

That Sunday night I called Mother, remembering what she had once said about a pastor at her church. I told her about the weekend's ordeal, how I had called out to God for help, and that I had vowed I would believe in him if he helped me. The next morning Mother made an appointment for me to see the pastoral counselor at the Hope Presbyterian Church, Rev. Allan Talley. Three days later I sat nervously awaiting my first visit with Pastor Talley.

Allan Talley was unlike most men I knew. He demanded nothing from me and did not see me for his own self-interests. Instead, he only wished to help me experience wholeness. He asked for little in return for his hours of counseling, only that I be open and receptive to the claims of Jesus and the Bible. He was giving, gentle, and sensitive as he probed and searched to help me sort out all my feelings, thoughts, and fears. He genuinely cared about me in spite of my past offenses, and he wanted to see me restored in body, soul, and spirit through the healing power of the love of Christ. Rev. Talley was the bridge over the troubled waters of my life that would lead me to Jesus.

Throughout my early visits to Pastor Talley, I cried incessantly, as all my guilt, bitterness, and disappointments came to the surface. I poured out my longings to him, and he comforted me with words of wisdom—counsel based on biblical principles. My weekly visit with him was the most important hour in my life. It gave me a distinct reason to live and a hope I'd never known before.

By the end of my fourth visit with Allan I felt sure I could trust him. I was finally convinced that he really did care for me. During those one-hour sessions he made me feel significant and worthy of love, and I clung to that desperately. After that fourth session, he sensed my dependence on him and as I got up to leave, he pulled a picture out of his desk drawer and handed it to me. It was a picture of Jesus praying.

"Sandy, it's good for you to talk to me each week like this," he said as he leaned back on his swivel chair. "But I can't always be around. Jesus can be with you forever, and he'll always listen when you talk to him."

I sat down again and looked at the picture of a rough and rugged Jesus with his eyes closed and hands folded, praying. He looked so

Jewish, unlike so many pictures I'd seen of him with fair skin and sandy hair.

"Put the picture in your home, Sandy, and share with Jesus as you do with me. Tell him everything and then listen for him to speak to you."

"How does Jesus speak?" I questioned.

"Often through a still, small voice," Allan replied.

"My friends always told me that Jesus wasn't for the Jews," I said somewhat defensively. "They said Jesus was responsible for the deaths of many Jewish people, such as in the Crusades, or the Spanish Inquistion, when Christians killed Jews because of Jesus."

"Sandy, our history is full of horror and bloodshed because of humanity's lack of love. Although the Crusaders believed they were doing God's will, they had forgotten that Jesus' greatest commandment was to love. The cross of Christ has been used to sanction many bloody deeds. But we can't accuse Jesus for the wrongdoing of those who carried his name. Christians who understand the true power of Jesus' love have no part in anti-Semitism. They love the Jewish people because they know the Bible and Jesus came through the Jews."

I remembered Bob's distraught voice at the mere mention of Jesus' name. "Mother told me about Jesus," I continued, "but I didn't want to hear because I was angry at Mother and because I wanted to be like Father who didn't believe in a God. Then Bob took Father's place and Bob insisted that our children be raised in a Jewish home, so I turned off the Jesus idea completely. Yes, I'll pray to Jesus and talk to him, Allan, but I need a sign to know for sure that Jesus is God. Does that make sense?"

"The Bible frequently mentions signs. As a matter of fact, it says that the Jews often require a sign. Why don't you pray for it?"

For a long moment I looked quietly at Allan Talley. I had been afraid that he would grow to dislike me as I shared with him the ugliness of my life—all the drinking, pills, and the men I'd known, not to mention all the buried hate and bitterness I felt toward so many people. And yet, the more he learned of me the more he seemed to care about me as a person. I reasoned that if Allan could really know what I was like and still love me despite my failures, then he had to be empowered with a supernatural love. And if that supernatural ability came from Jesus, then I wanted to look into it.

At Allan's suggestion I began attending Sunday morning services at the Hope Presbyterian Church. Or rather, I attended whenever I didn't have a bad hangover from a Saturday night drinking binge. My life style really didn't change during the first few weeks of my sessions with Allan.

My first Sunday in a Christian church was an experience. I felt insecure and embarrassed to be there, though I was surrounded by an atmosphere of love and acceptance. I sat in the back row and kept my sunglasses on the whole time. I felt awkward because I was overdressed

in my elegant cocktail dress. I hadn't had a
drink before church that morning, hoping my
discipline would make me feel more spiritual,
but my craving for a drink prevented me from
concentrating on the sermon. For the next
several Sundays I came back, but frequently left
before the service ended in order to go home to
have a drink. My motivation to attend church
was to please Allan Talley and not to hear about
God or Jesus.

One of Allan's primary concerns was my
bondage to Satan as a result of involvement in
astrology. I knew little about Satan and had a
hard enough time accepting a God-concept.

"Maybe God is behind the astrology
signs?" I questioningly said to Allan the next
week, hoping to defend my amusing pastime.

He opened his well-worn Bible to a Scrip-
ture passage. "Sorry, Sandy. God forbids it. Let
me read you a verse or two from Deuteronomy.
'There shall not be found among you any one
that maketh his son or his daughter to pass
through the fire, or that useth divination, or an
observer of times, or an enchanter, or a witch.
Or a charmer, or a consulter with familiar
spirits, or a wizard, or a necromancer. For all
that do these things are an abomination unto the
Lord: and because of these abominations the
Lord thy God doth drive them out from before
thee' (Deut. 18:10-12)." Allan looked up and
realized that I didn't fully understand.

"In biblical terminology an astrologist
would be called an 'observer of times' and a
'consulter with familiar spirits.' Astrology is

definitely a part of the occult experience that God warns against. And anyone who participates in the occult, no matter how innocent it seems, opens himself to the satanic influence of witchcraft."

"But they didn't have astrological horoscopes way back then, did they?" I protested.

"In the book of Daniel, a reference is made to King Nebuchadnezzar who summoned his magicians, wizards, sorcerers, and astrologers to help him interpret a dream. Astrology was very popular in his culture, and it developed from a pagan Babylonian belief that each star was a god who exercised control over people's lives. We can't put our future into the hands of the stars. We must put our future into the hands of God alone."

"But the horoscopes were right many times," I argued. "Does that mean that it was just coincidence?"

"I believe Satan can only predict what he can cause, Sandy. And he's caused a great deal to happen in your life. Do you think your alcoholism and drug addiction were from God? Playing with any form of the occult is not resisting the devil—it is assisting him."

Since astrology and horoscopes had become such a regular part of my day, I wasn't about to part with them without a struggle.

"I feel a pull to the horoscopes like I do to brushing my teeth. It's a natural part of my day. How can I give up something that is a part of me?"

Allan's face lit up as he warmed to the subject I had unwittingly allowed him to expound on. "Sandy, you can only attain victory over this if you ask Jesus to come into your life and take complete control. Jesus will fill your heart with his love, and his power, if you ask him to. With Jesus as your source of strength, you can be truly at peace for the first time in your life! He says in the book of John that he, Jesus, has come to give us the abundant life. That's abundance apart from all the things you think you need—liquor, horoscopes . . . even men."

Allan Talley's words remained with me throughout the next week. They seemed to be engraved on my mind and no amount of effort could drive them out. It occurred to me that perhaps God was speaking to me through that still, small voice Allan told me about.

And yet, my working situation was full of temptation. How could I free myself from my wants and desires? I couldn't give up my job, and yet it thrust me into a position in which I was bound to receive attention from available men. I had access to all of the membership files, and I learned all the vital "statistics" on the single men. I learned their names and their interests, and then showed them special attention that was entirely self-motivated. It was just manipulation to gain their friendship, attention, or love. The drinking lunches and dinners kept on, and I felt as though I had a foot in two worlds. There was definitely a foot in the spiritual realm, though at this point I was only searching. And I couldn't deny that I was still thoroughly enmeshed in the attractions of my everyday world.

But instead of acccepting Jesus, I resorted to heavier drinking. I drank so much I hardly ate, and I looked pale and thin, requiring a quart of alcohol a day to function. I searched for a bottle of vodka before I brushed my teeth in the morning. My emotions kept me on the proverbial roller coaster, as I soared to the heights after a session with Allan Talley, and later that week broke every promise I had made to Allan and to Jesus.

During my search God brought Calvin Lundberg to me. He was a member of the health club and a Edina police officer. Calvin told me early in our friendship that he was a "born-again" Christian. He reversed roles with me, and unlike all the other men, he questioned me and listened to me. He seemed happily married and I was sure that his interest in me was not selfish. Now I had Cal and Allan hitting me several times a week with this "born-again" idea, but in a soft-spoken, non-preachy manner. Their very lives evidenced a love and a peace I couldn't ignore, and their words continually rang in my ears. "Born again" people seemed to be beautiful people, and I always wanted to be with them, though secretly I felt Jesus couldn't forgive some of my sins.

One morning as I studied the horoscopes for the day, my eye caught a glimpse of something. On a line in print so fine it was hardly readable I saw that Bob Abrams had remarried. I had been sure that my feelings for

Bob had been dealt with during sessions with Allan. I had forgiven Bob and thought I could finally let go of him. But now my bitterness, resentment, and pain surfaced once again, and I felt I was right back where I started.

FOURTEEN
Born Again!

Subconsciously, I had retained a hope for reconciliation with Bob, but now my secret yearning was destroyed. The semblance of self-worth I had been able to muster was dashed now that Bob had chosen to love another woman. I felt that if I had been attractive, then Bob would have wanted me. But he didn't. And no amount of counseling could pick me up this time. It was just the final blow, and I didn't seem to have any further reason to live.

I walked into the kitchen, fully aware of my intention to find a sharp knife. Just a quick thrust into my flesh, and my suffering would be over. It didn't matter that my children would come home and find the macabre scene. All that mattered was putting an end to the hurt inside of me.

I put the knife to my heart and wanted to push the blade in, but something held me back and the knife clattered to the floor. I tumbled to the kitchen floor after it and wept over my bungled plan and cowardice. I sat weeping for a moment, then cried out in desperation.

"O God, help me. Jesus, if you exist, help me now." I expected no answer, but within seconds after I cried out, the doorbell rang. I decided to go to the door, and even if it was just the paper boy, I could pour out my heart to him.

Cal Lundberg stood on my front steps, dressed in his blue police uniform. I tried to smile through the tears as I opened the screen door.

"Cal, what are you doing here?"

"I was driving down France Avenue, Sandy, and the Lord sent me over here. He said you needed help just now. May I come in?"

"You didn't have my address, did you?" I was astonished at this communication between God and Cal.

"No, I didn't, but the Lord directed me right to your home. I know something is wrong. If I could come in, perhaps we could pray together."

As Cal walked into the living room, I realized that I felt perfectly safe with him, and I was touched by his sensitivity to me and my predicament. I told him that I had just learned of Bob's remarriage, and how my dreams had been shattered. I also told Cal of my intentions to take my life.

"Sandy, if you would just let Jesus into your life, he would give you the strength to cope with these things. He wants you to trust him completely so he can turn everything that appears to be a tragedy into a triumph."

As Cal talked, he seemed to sense my fears and apprehension. I felt as if he could even see the feelings I thought I had so carefully hidden.

"Sandy, you think that Jesus won't forgive you, don't you? But Jesus says that 'If we confess our sins, he is faithful and just to forgive us our sins, and to cleanse us . . . ' (1 John 1:9). No sin is too foul for God to forgive, and no sinner is beyond God's love and saving grace. God wants to forgive you for your attempt to take your life. We could pray right now and ask him to forgive you, if you like."

"I can't pray, Cal, but you can pray for me." My voice sounded shaky as I struggled to keep my emotions under control. "You can ask him to forgive me for what I tried to do, but I'm just not ready to wholeheartedly accept Jesus as the answer to my problems."

Cal prayed for me and asked God to forgive my thoughts and actions. He also entreated God to show me my need of a Savior, through the Holy Spirit. It still didn't make much sense to me, but Cal was so loving and concerned that I was willing to listen to anything he said.

During the week Allan Talley encouraged me to make a special effort to come to church Sunday. That Sunday, Easter, 1972, Dr. Louis Evans was to be the guest speaker and Allan was sure that Dr. Evans would be especially inspiring to me. I promised Allan I would be there, and felt that perhaps it would ease some of the disappointment he had in me. I hadn't read the Bible he'd given me, and I was ashamed to tell him of my attempted suicide.

I was late for church that Sunday morning. Unfortunately, my spot in the back row had been filled as well as every single seat in the sanctuary except for two folding chairs in the front row. Reluctantly, I let myself be escorted by the usher down to the front of the auditorium. But as I sat there, I had the distinct feeling that the chair next to me was occupied by an unseen presence.

I deliberately didn't drink before church that morning, and my usual symptoms didn't set in. Even the anticipation of the symptoms left my thoughts and I was able to give full attention to Dr. Louis Evans.

Dr. Evans used some of the same language I'd heard in recent weeks. He spoke of Jesus dying to give us the abundant life on earth and eternal life after death. He said if we placed our trust in Jesus and allowed him control, we would no longer find ourselves living lives of futility and desperation. We only excluded ourselves from God's family by not allowing Jesus to love us, touch us, and heal us. He said no sin was bad enough to exclude us from God's family.

Maybe it was a strange rationalization, but what did I have to lose if I gave my life to Jesus? And to hear Allan, Cal, and Dr. Evans speak, I had everything to gain, for Jesus specialized in transforming lives.

When Dr. Evans finished his message, he asked those who wanted to make Jesus the Lord and Savior of their lives to stand. I heard some folding chairs shuffle as many stood that morning. I felt two spirits at war within me— urging me in two different directions. One force tried to pull me out of the chair and another told me to remain seated, for I was not worthy of Jesus' love and forgiveness. But I soon gave in to the desire to accept Jesus and allow him to straighten out my life. It had been easy for me to turn my life over to external influences like drugs and alcohol, but it was much harder for me to ask an unseen God to come into my life. And yet I couldn't deny that the force that prompted me to seek Jesus in the first place was more than just coincidence. Jesus had to be for real, and I wanted him to make me into a new person. Perhaps Jesus could help me to be warm and loving like Allan Tailey and Cal Lundberg.

Dr. Evans led in a prayer which we all repeated. It was a simple prayer asking God to forgive us and to allow his Son, Jesus, to come into our lives and take complete control. As I uttered the prayer I felt released from my guilt and despondency, and I experienced a peace that could only have come from God.

The air was still cool as I left the church that Easter Sunday morning. As I stepped out into the church parking lot, I barely noticed the crisp breeze or the patches of snow under my feet, for I felt like I was floating on a cloud. I felt free! Lifted! Released! I wanted to shout excitedly, "I just received Jesus into my life!" The only way I could describe this feeling was to associate it with the way I would feel if I had lost eighty pounds without a diet. Besides, at least eighty pounds of sin rolled off of me that day.

God turned my mourning into dancing (Eccl. 3:4), for I had been born again!

FIFTEEN
He Touched Me!

God gave me less than an hour before he tested my commitment. Bob called after I got home from church and asked to have the children for the day. He wanted them to meet Marilyn, his new wife. I quickly prayed and asked Jesus to show me what to do or say in the situation. Not only did Jesus prod me to let the children go for the day, but he even seemed to be saying that I must show a special love for Bob and Marilyn.

The children were delighted to hear that they would spend the day with their father. I thought back to the days when I had grieved Mother's heart because I wanted to be with Father, and I felt sad that I had caused her the pain I now felt.

Twenty minutes later Bob and Marilyn drove up. As they walked up the front sidewalk my heart sank. She was beautiful and could easily have been a cover girl. My new radiance vanished and the old feelings of rejection surfaced. I was sure Bob had left me because I wasn't attractive enough, and I had always felt that my appearance was the one thing I had going for me. Now that fantasy was crushed.

The introductions were awkward, but I put in an Oscar-winning performance. I couldn't let Bob and Marilyn see how my life had been affected by their marriage. If anything, I wanted to begin showing them that I now had something special worth living for, but as the five of them left moments later I heard an inner voice say to me, "Why didn't Jesus give you the strength to be happy with this situation? Don't you see that he has failed you?"

I tried to suppress that nagging voice and I cried out to Jesus to comfort me. I reached for the fail-safe comforter in the liquor cabinet, but as I raised a glass of vodka to my mouth, my hand shot down and the glass shattered on the kitchen floor. I reached for another glass and poured a second drink and waited for some calming effect to take place.

In my weakened situation, I knew it would not be good for me to be alone. So I called Cal, then Allan Talley, and then Mother, but got no answer. I remembered that Kathy, my next door neighbor, was a Christian. She had shared Christ with me occasionally, but as with everyone else, I let much of it go in one ear and out the other. It occurred to me that I could go over to her house and talk to her for awhile.

I called Kathy and told her of my commitment to Jesus that day, and of the disappointment that had followed less than two hours afterward.

"Sandy, God is just testing you to see if you can let go and trust him for everything," Kathy explained. "After nearly every promise made to God, there is a test to see if we meant it. Did you mean it today when you gave your life to Jesus?"

"I think so," I mumbled through some tears. "But I was sure some of the problems would ease up."

"Sandy, come over here this afternoon. I'll fix some iced tea and we can talk about it, OK?"

A few moments later I sat with Kathy at her kitchen table, sipping tea and listening carefully as she tried to encourage me. Why couldn't Jesus make the burden of my broken marriage go away?

"The life of the Christian isn't a carefree fantasy world, Sandy," Kathy said as I nervously poked at the ice in my glass. "It's full of heartaches, but eventually we look back on them and see how they ultimately worked out for good in our lives. Maybe things happen to teach us a lesson, or to build character in us. Or maybe what's happening to us seems a tragedy, but an all-knowing God can turn that disappointment into victory."

"I know my faith is weak," I admitted. "But I've always needed a confirmation of things. I've always needed someone or something to affirm my decisions. Call it a sign or whatever. I believe my commitment to Jesus was real today, but do you think it hurts to ask for a confirmation?''

"Why don't we ask God right now to reveal himself to you in a unique way," Kathy replied.

Kathy prayed for several minutes. She prayed so positively that I could tell she really believed God would answer her prayer. She was sure that God wanted to bless my life abundantly.

We sat at the kitchen table for another hour after we had prayed. Kathy continued to encourage me and shared some Bible verses that she wanted me to memorize. I listened carefully and jotted down the Bible references.

Suddenly, as Kathy spoke, the room darkened. She was less than three feet away from me, but she was obscured by an unbelievable midday blackout. I wanted to call out or at least leave the room, but I experienced an uncanny inability to get up from my chair.

I felt an arm on my shoulder. What on earth was happening? I looked to one side and saw someone standing next to me in a long, white garment, and at the bottom emerged two sandaled feet. The feet had marks in them as though they had at one time been pierced by nails or spikes. A compassionate voice spoke.

"Sandy, don't be afraid and don't let your heart be troubled. Only believe in me."

I turned to look up at the man whose voice I heard, but he was gone. In an instant it was over and the light returned to the kitchen. I knew I had seen Jesus! Did I dare label this just a bizarre vision or a hallucination of a mixed-up alcoholic woman? Though I didn't see his face, I knew I'd seen the nail-scarred feet of Jesus, and I knew that he had chosen to reveal himself to me and give me that sign I needed. Jesus knew what it would take to confirm my faith and make it stronger!

"What on earth happened to you?" questioned Kathy. She had seen nothing and had not experienced the total darkness.

"It was Jesus! He was here in this room with us. He stood by me and told me not to be afraid!"

"I watched you and I knew you saw something. Your expression was marvelous, Sandy. Whatever was happening, I knew it was special."

"I'm going to make it now," I announced. I got up and gave Kathy a hug. "Things will work out, I know. God gave me the sign I asked for. How can I doubt anything now, Kathy? He touched me. He actually touched me!"

SIXTEEN
I'll Shout It from the Mountaintops

I still didn't acknowledge the convicting power of the Holy Spirit, and I continued to drink. After I left Kathy's that afternoon I had several drinks, and the next morning I opened the day with my usual amount of liquor. But I couldn't deny obvious changes, such as an even greater love for my children. Even the remaining remnants of jealousy over Bob's love for our daughter Stephanie disappeared, and in its place I had the most all-encompassing new love for her. I was able to take on a new attitude toward Bob and Marilyn and show them more love. My appreciation and fondness for my stepdad, Leonard, grew, and I saw qualities in him that made me love him as a real father. My smiling countenance was a delightfully new experience for people who had been so used to seeing my usual expression of rejection and self-pity. But perhaps the newest thing in my life was my desire to share Jesus with everyone!

The morning after Jesus touched me, I called seven girl friends and shared my experience with them. All of them were Jewish, and they received my news with real disinterest. In so many words they said it was fine for me, but Jesus wasn't for them, nor would he ever be. He was the God of the Gentiles. I never heard from any of them again.

Tuesday morning I was back at the health club wanting to share Christ with everyone. Men gathered around my desk to hear how Jesus had changed my life. Several of the men told me that they, too, had accepted Jesus into their lives, and wondered why so few of them had ever told me about it. I was learning that every Christian is not an enthusiastic propagator of the faith.

One of the men with whom I shared my story was Chip Atkinson. He told me that two weeks earlier he, too, had given his life to Jesus. Would I join him for dinner so that we might share our experiences?

The next evening Chip picked me up and I could hardly wait to talk about the Lord with him. He was so unlike all the other dates I'd had. I became so caught up in conversation about Jesus with Chip that I hardly thought about my dinner. Again, how unlike me!

Out of habit, I ordered several drinks that night with Chip. After I ordered my fourth Black Russian, Chip finally interrupted me.

"You know, Sandy, I did a lot of drinking before I became a Christian. But when I asked

Jesus into my life I asked him to take the place of all the crutches I had been leaning on. The first was alcohol. I read in 2 Corinthians 6 that our bodies are the temple of God and that we shouldn't defile that temple with anything that could be really dangerous to our health."

I felt awkward, for there was so much about this Christian life that I didn't understand. I felt like a stranger in another country and I was afraid that everything I did might be wrong and offensive.

"Tell me why you drink, anyway," Chip asked. He had no idea I was an alcoholic.

"I guess I drink out of habit, Chip. For years it has given me confidence. But I can quit any time, of course." The lie I had just told made me squirm a bit, and I hoped Chip wouldn't sense my uneasiness.

"Of course, now you can totally rely on Jesus," Chip replied.

"Sure," I answered enthusiastically. I was uncomfortable with my game as a con artist.

We talked until the restaurant closed. The ride home was unusually quiet, but then we had talked ourselves out earlier that evening. In the quiet of that late-night ride home, God spoke to me again. Perhaps it was that still, small voice I'd heard about. I was told simply, "Now that you have accepted me, Sandy, you have two choices. You can continue to drink and ruin your life, or you can stop now and someday marry the man sitting next to you."

How absurd! I'd known Chip Atkinson less than five hours, and God was telling me I could marry him! How could I even know if he were interested in me and my three children?

God, I prayed, if this message is from you, give me a sign. I must know that the words aren't the insecure thoughts of a lonely divorcee, thinking secret dreams are words out of Heaven. Just a small sign, Lord.

As Chip brought me to the door that night he made a casual statement. "Sandy, I'd like to get to know your children a little. May I spend some time with them this week?"

O God, you just don't waste a minute, do you? You're never taking a vacation, floating on some celestial cloud detached from our lives, are you? Indeed, it was your voice I heard moments earlier. God, you've been a miracle-worker in my life, long before I ever knew you existed. Now here's my biggest request, Lord. Help me never to take a drink again. Dear Jesus, I will dread seeing the light of morning, but you and I are going to make it together, aren't we? Uphold me, God, through the next several days.

SEVENTEEN
Cold Turkey

When morning arrived I reluctantly crawled out of bed, wishing I could turn back the clock to delay the inevitable symptoms. I dreaded the many hours of discomfort ahead of me. Fortunately, it was my day off and the boys would be in school all day. My neighbor took Stephanie to nursery school, so for a few hours at least, I could battle withdrawal alone.

By 7:30 A.M. I felt the need of a drink. The sight of food on the breakfast table nauseated me and I pushed Mark and Ross out the door for school a little early so they wouldn't have to see me even mildly ill.

I had no idea what to expect, or how long it would take me to get over the withdrawal symptoms. I thought of calling Allan Talley, Cal, or Mother to have them pray for me, but I was afraid they would want to come over. Right now, I just wanted to be alone and avoid further embarrassment while I dried out.

The symptoms were slow in coming, and as with everything else, I wanted to hurry up and be done with it. By midday I lay down, overcome by nausea and a headache, and by 6:00 that evening the whole gamut of chills, vomiting, body aches, and headache had hit me with full force. I told the children that I had the flu and asked Mark to tell Chip that when he called later that night.

By 10:00 that night I was so weak from vomiting that I couldn't even make it to the bathroom without help. Mark came and sat by my side, putting a wet rag on my forehead every few minutes or helping me to the bathroom. Throughout the night everything worsened and I had the dry heaves. I couldn't imagine a killer plague more unpleasant than this, and a hundred times I thought of breaking my promise to God. Why couldn't I be a Christian and still drink? I could learn to drink in moderation, and it would be no more sinful than overeating. If God wanted me dry, surely he could ease the discomfort. Satan pounded me with doubts and questions.

Mark stayed by my side that whole night and throughout the next day. I was so sick I lapsed into seconds of near-insanity and threw two ceramic knick-knacks across the room. Then I got down on my knees and prayed that God would help me. Chip had called and had spoken to Mark, and shortly thereafter Chip came over to be with the children during my illness.

I felt very alone, for I couldn't share with anyone what was really happening to me. I could only speak to God, and I alternated between praying and shaking my fist at him for making this project so difficult. If I had had the strength, I would have checked myself into a hospital and dried out much less painfully, as I had the last time. But that meant giving in, drinking some liquor to make it to the hospital, and then starting over again.

The symptoms continued through the second night and into the third day—nausea, dry heaves, body aches, and a monstrous headache. Midmorning of the third day, Chip came over again. He still didn't know that my symptoms were withdrawal from liquor, but he prepared a remedy for me that he was sure could help. He mixed apple cider vinegar with honey and water and felt that it could combat the flu-like symptoms. I later learned that such a mixture was often helpful to an alcoholic coming off liquor. The body that has been drinking large amounts of alcohol craves potassium, and the vinegar takes care of that craving and serves as a tonic as well as a relaxer. The honey helps the craving for sugar that was provided by the alcohol.

Within an hour after Chip gave me the drink, the symptoms eased. When I asked him later where he got the idea, he said that he felt the Lord had given him the formula to ease the flu-like symptoms. Chip wouldn't find out for some time that I was an alcoholic. That third night I finally slept and I realized I had to work the next day, as I had already missed a full day.

I knew my first day back at the health club would be the longest day of my life. I had conquered the physical need for the alcohol, but now I had to mentally and emotionally cope without it for the entire day. I was tired and weak physically and mentally and knew I was incapable of coping with the slightest pressure at work.

That first day back at the club I realized how dependent I had been on the alcohol. Every smile and gracious hello had been stimulated by the liquor. Every pressure and tension had been bearable because of it. Every artificial comment or gesture sounded sincere as long as I was fortified night and day with the alcohol. How could I now maintain that pleasant, outgoing personality that the job required? Years of pills, alcohol, or both had created a false front that had fooled even me.

That first day back at the club dragged on forever. I seldom took my eyes off the clock and prayed that God would speed up the day. Every thought, action, and smile was forced. I couldn't even share Jesus that day, but I knew he would understand. During my lunch break I took a long walk to get away from any unpleasantries that made my thoughts turn to liquor. I turned down a luncheon invitation because I was sure it would be in a setting that would tempt me.

But at 6:00 that evening I walked through my back door and knew I'd made it—an eleven-hour workday and no drinks! The atmosphere and conversation at the club had always driven me to the comfort of liquor in the past because it made me feel like I belonged in nearly every situation. That day had been a very important victory.

The acid test was over. But I still had a very strong desire to drink, so from now on I'd have to trust God to help me stay dry. I would have to depend on him minute by minute to keep from ever indulging again in "just one little drink."

EIGHTEEN
The Truth
Will Set
You Free

The temptation to give in and take a drink
nagged at me constantly. Commercials,
billboards, and newspaper ads screamed at me.
Old friends drank in front of me. I gained
weight quickly, and nothing could so easily drive
me to desperation. In the past whenever I had
seen the scale inch slightly higher, I had
automatically resorted to pills and liquor to hold
it down. Now I found it necessary to be in constant prayer over my continued desire to drink,
and I also sought help from Allan Talley.

I continued to keep a cupboard full of
liquor in the house "just in case." One particularly desperate moment came when
Stephanie, who had reached the age of five, was
home with me. I told her that the liquor was
medicine and that I needed to have some, but
her alert and perceptive mind realized that I was
not ill. Her piercing and convicting words, "But

Mommy, you feel fine," showed me that I couldn't give in to my disastrous urge. Two days later Chip discovered the alcohol I'd kept hidden and poured $200 worth of liquor down my sink. I was furious, yet at the same time somewhat relieved, for it had been a constant source of temptation.

I talked to God continually, and thanked him for the support he'd given me in people like Allan Talley, Cal and Elaine Lundberg, Chip, and Mother. Chip and I began to attend church regularly and to seek out the fellowship of other Christians from whom we could gain strength. I wanted my children, now thirteen, nine, and five, to learn about Jesus, so I brought them to a nearby Baptist church and enrolled them in the Sunday school program.

But it seemed the temptation to resort to liquor always nagged at me. I couldn't understand why God would allow me to continually be in situations that were a temptation! Chip and I visited his parents at their beautiful home in Canada. I knew how wealthy they were and I felt that my lack of self-confidence in this situation would necessitate drinking to sustain my composure. When we arrived I saw that not only could I not cope with the life style of the very wealthy, I also couldn't cope with the constant round of drinking.

Chip still didn't know I was an alcoholic and didn't realize the incredible temptation I was subjected to as I watched martinis, and a whole assortment of other alcoholic beverages, float by me for an entire week. A cocktail was never more than three feet away. I was so nervous and apprehensive I was afraid his parents wouldn't approve of me, but when they did approve, I felt certain God must have blinded them to my insecurities. As we returned to Minneapolis I was sure that I had passed God's testing and that I was now home free. But that would hardly be the case.

When I arrived home I received a message to call Father in California. My grandmother was dying and she had asked me to come and see her. This meant more testing, for I would be with a whole host of people who would continually be asking me to drink. I felt that this time the temptation would be beyond my level to endure. Father always drank too much and he would be asking me to join him. Old memories would haunt me and I'd desire to drink simply to forget my unhappy past. Could I really trust God in this situation and cast all my care on him? Why couldn't God let my testing with Chip's parents be satisfactory? Why throw me from that proverbial frying pan into the fire?

I felt I had to tell Chip the whole story so that he, Allan, Cal, and Mother could pray for me as I went to California. It seemed that all my life I had hidden some of the facts from the people closest to me. Moments later I telephoned Chip and stumbled over my confession.

"I have always lived a half-truth, Chip," I confessed. "When I was a kid I stole money for candy and donuts. When I was with Bob I tried to make him think I was on diet pills and not speed. And I've tried to keep from you, Chip, the fact that I'm an alcoholic and that I have drunk more than a quart of liquor a day even after I met you. I was going through withdrawal the week you thought I had the flu. Can you ever forgive me for being such a con artist, Chip?"

"Well, Sandy, your act was very convincing because I didn't suspect a thing. Of course I forgive you. And don't you see? You're free now just like the Bible says in John 8:32—'and you shall know the truth, and the truth shall make you free.' Confessing releases us from guilt. Don't you feel better for having said it to yourself and to me, Sandy?"

I really did feel better. It was such a relief not to be living a lie and having to dodge uncomfortable situations.

"The reason I've told you is that I must fly to California tomorrow, to see my grandmother. Father has asked me to come, and I know the booze will flow like a river. Please pray for me, Chip, and call Allan Talley and Cal Lundberg and ask them to pray. I'm calling Mother right now."

The next day I boarded the plane, took my seat by the window, and waited for the two other people who would occupy the seats beside me. Since Chip had kindly offered to take a week off from work to stay with Mark, Ross, and Stephanie, I knew the children would be well taken care of. So I settled in my seat, with my Bible in my lap, and turned my thoughts to Father, Grandmother, and California. Just then,

I heard the obnoxious giggles of a hip, young, and vivacious girl as she moved toward her seat. I looked very startled and dismayed when she arrived at my seat. I had hoped she'd walk on past. However, she plopped down with a crash in the seat right next to me while several of her small packages toppled onto me. As she awkwardly apologized and rearranged things, I thought: Why couldn't I get a traveling partner who would keep to herself and allow me to get my thoughts together?

"Hi, I'm Gloria!" she announced to me enthusiastically.

"I'm Sandy Abrams." I hoped that after the introductions the conversation would fall flat, but she kept talking.

"I'm going to meet my boyfriend in L.A.," she explained proudly as she strapped herself in. "Well, actually we've never met. I began writing to him in the service and we kind of fell in love by letter. Can you believe it?"

I tried to show interest in her story until she was interrupted by our third seat-mate. I hoped that he would occupy Gloria's attention so I could relax, but instead, he only made matters worse. He was the stereotypical back-slapping used-car salesman who wanted the world to know that he had made it big against all odds. As he blew cigar smoke in our faces he introduced himself as Ralph, Mr. Big, Salesman of the Year, who was definitely going places.

Ralph leaned over and boastfully announced, "Ladies, I want to celebrate today. I just set a record in sales this year. I'm due for a promotion and it will be a big one this time. Now I want you two charming ladies to celebrate with me on this long trip to California. The drinks are on me, and there is no limit. Anything you want, big Ralph here will provide by way of beverage delight and refreshment. Now don't be bashful. That nice young stewardess over there will be here in a few moments and I want to turn in an order for three drinks. What will it be, ladies?"

O dear God, what have you done? Just how strong do you think I am? I wanted to leave the plane, but just then it began to taxi down the runway. *O Jesus, help me out of this!* I cautiously glanced around, hoping to find another vacant seat, but my heart sank as I saw none.

Gloria let out a scream of delight. She was thrilled with her drinking partner and I knew the suds would fly between the two of them. Why me, Lord? Why was I sitting next to the two people—out of 150 passengers—who would obviously drink themselves to oblivion?

Gloria and Ralph looked at me, obviously irritated. "So what's with you?" Gloria asked, seeing my obvious lack of response. "I mean, you're sitting there like you're frozen to your seat."

"I am?" I tried to look casual but only felt more awkward. Perhaps they would be more understanding if I candidly explained my situation.

Gloria was continuing. "How many times does a handsome gentleman like Ralph here, who is Salesman of the Year, no less, make such a generous offer?'' Gloria looked at Ralph affectionately as she spoke.

The plane roared down the runway, and that momentarily diverted their attention. Moments later the stewardess stood over us and asked the inevitable question: "Can I get you a drink today?"

"You bet you can," Ralph blurted out obnoxiously. "A martini for me and this lovely young lady, and this lady will have a . . ." There was a long pause as they waited for my choice of a drink. Who would know if I took a drink? It took all my willpower to keep from blurting out "vodka and 7-Up."

"Uh, nothing I guess."

Gloria looked on in unbelief. "Nothing?" she questioned.

"Well, you see, I'm an alcoholic." There. I had finally said it. Several awkward seconds of silence followed. Then Gloria finally broke in.

"Don't worry, Sandy. I have a brother who is an alcoholic. Ralph and I won't let you drink a thing, will we, Ralph?"

And drink they did. The drinks were refilled nonstop for an hour. They were both getting high and silly, and I prayed that God would make this scene more bearable. Gloria would set her drink down just inches from me and I would stare at the liquor in her glass. It looked so tempting.

During their second hour of drinking Gloria began to feel ill, but she couldn't pass up the free drinks and didn't quit. Ralph was delighted to have her admiring attention and coaxed her to keep going. Even the stewardess tried to be polite in suggesting Gloria quit.

The giggles finally stopped and Gloria's face turned a sickly shade. She looked at me with blurry eyes and said, "Sandy, I'm going to the ladies' room because I don't feel well. Would you hold my drink for me?"

She didn't wait for an answer, but plunked down her martini on my lap so that it sat right on my Bible. She stumbled over Ralph and dashed to the restroom. As I looked silently at the drink balanced on my lap, I thought: *God, is this a joke?* Surely, you must be kidding. But, God, I believe you're in control, and somehow you have allowed this temptation. Just don't forget, God, you promised you wouldn't tempt me beyond my limit!

I looked at the drink for several minutes and could have imagined that a horned creature with a pitchfork tail grinned back at me from inside the glass. If I could only open the Bible—but that meant putting my hand to the glass, which surely meant putting it to my lips.

I asked God for a miracle just then, one that would take away my desire to sip that drink. Why was Gloria taking so long? Ten minutes passed . . . wasn't that sufficient test, Lord? Ten minutes stretched to twenty. Why couldn't Ralph dig up an ounce of understanding and take the drink from its precarious position?

Jesus, take away this awful temptation, I prayed. I thought the truth would set me free, so why hasn't it, Lord?

After thirty minutes I heard the familiar laughter from Gloria and I knew she was on her way back. She stumbled over Ralph and plopped herself down next to me. "Gee, thanks, Sandy," she said as she took the drink from my lap and sat back refreshed and renewed for nearly two more hours of alcoholic gluttony.

I leaned back and breathed a sigh of relief. I felt somewhat drained from the ordeal, but I knew I had gained the victory in yet another battle. Now, as I relaxed, my thoughts drifted to Father and the many years it had been since we'd seen each other. So much had happened, but my special love for him hadn't faded. It had just been shoved into the background of my tumultuous life. Now in less than an hour we would land in L.A. I was so very happy now—happy to have met Jesus and pleased with my deliverance from pills, alcohol, and the overwhelming self-hate I'd known for so many years. And I had a hope . . . a hope for better days ahead. The nagging thought that Father would drink in front of me and would want me to drink with him was just another area in which I must trust God completely. Since God had given me strength through the testing on the plane, he could certainly help me with my father.

As I caught sight of Father after deplaning, I noticed he had changed little since we had seen each other nearly twelve years ago. He hadn't lost his handsome appearance but had acquired a few additional gray hairs and deeper lines in his face. His warm embrace seemed to close the gap between the years since we'd last been together. But my struggle with alcohol surfaced immediately, for Father's first few words were, "Let's go and get a drink, Sandy. We have a lot to catch up on." God's testing of me seemed relentless.

"I can't, Dad, I'm an alcoholic." There, I had said it again.

"Don't be ridiculous, Sandy. We've never had an alcoholic in our family." He was offended and didn't believe me.

"Dad, I drank a quart of liquor a day for ten years. I wasn't able to function in life without it."

Father didn't respond and wasn't convinced, but he dropped the idea of us getting a drink together. On the way to the house Father outlined the plan for the week in California. Except for visits with my grandmother, many of the activities included drinking. I knew I would be in situations in which it would be awkward and embarrassing to Father for me to decline a cocktail.

That night in my room I got down on my knees and prayed for strength for the coming week. I prayed so long that I fell asleep on my knees, but I felt assured that God would get me through the week. However, I asked for a confirmation of that in some special way. God had always been so good in giving me special signs— and those signs made the arduous tests endurable.

Between hospital visits I spent every moment with Father. He always seemed to have a drink in his hand, and he took me to places where drinks were readily available. Each night I came home and got back down on my knees; it's a wonder I didn't develop calluses on them!

On the third morning I received a long-distance call from Chip. I braced myself for ominous news, but instead, I detected hints of surprise in Chip's voice.

"Sandy, something happened last night that we wanted to share with you. I'll let Mark tell you."

There was some shuffling as Chip handed the phone to Mark. I was nervous and Father looked at me curiously as I waited for the news. In the past such circumstances brought disaster and not good news.

"Hi, Mom. Me and Ross prayed to Jesus last night. We asked him into our lives. Chip wanted us to tell you today . . ."

Mark kept talking, but I'm not sure I heard much more than that. I knew I had received my sign again. What a victory! What perfect assurance that God would never fail me no matter how severe the test! The truth had set me free!

NINETEEN
Wall Street Becomes Our Wailing Wall

In the fall of 1973 the boys and I were baptized, and Stephanie prayed to receive Jesus. Shortly thereafter, Chip and I were married, and I could hardly believe God's goodness.

When we married, Chip was worth over a quarter of a million dollars. His parents had been in the garment business and his grandparents were instrumental in the Minnesota Mining and Manufacturing Company. We bought a nice home overlooking Minnehaha Creek, and though I felt some degree of financial freedom, something told me to keep my part-time job at the health club. Praise the Lord, I did, for the roof was about to fall in.

We hadn't been married two months when Chip came down with pneumonia. And while he lay helpless in bed, gradually our financial structure crumbled. The rapid series of tragic circumstances were timed with uncanny perfection. Phase one was word that the company for which he worked was closing its doors, putting Chip out of a job. He had invested money in several businesses, and with an eerie sense of timing, one by one those businesses failed. And through a series of unbelievable complications, his stock investments evaporated. But Chip was so ill with pneumonia that he was unable to dial a telephone to intercede.

For that eight-week period Chip was so sick I honestly felt God was going to take him away from me. He was alert enough, however, to estimate that in eight weeks' time we'd gone through $250,000, through absolutely no fault of our own.

I screamed at God over the injustice! Hadn't I paid my dues yet? Were happiness and security to be mine just long enough to enjoy the taste—only to be snatched away again?

It seemed God was asking us to put our trust in him completely, for in the few weeks I had been free from financial worry, I had again transferred my security to money. God was capable of feeding 5,000 with five loaves of bread and two fish, so surely he could take care of a family of five. The wages of a part-time receptionist would have to be multiplied, but I was learning that with God, anything is possible.

It was early December and I eagerly anticipated Christmas, for it would be my first year of appreciating the real significance of the holiday. In my innocent exuberance I had a desire to share the real meaning of Christmas with just about everyone. I decided to put up a sign on the health club bulletin board, with an appropriate Christmas message. This wasn't a typewritten three-by-five card, but a message in bold, two-inch-high letters. It read: "JESUS IS GOD'S CHRISTMAS GIFT OF LOVE TO US. IF YOU WOULD LIKE TO FIND OUT HOW YOU CAN KNOW JESUS PERSONALLY, PLEASE SEE SANDY."

The management had been upset with my previous efforts at evangelizing, but this was the last straw! I began to hear rumors that I might be replaced. Two weeks before Christmas the rumors were confirmed as the manager called me into her office.

"Sandy, we won't be needing you anymore. You can finish out the week if you like." Her words lacked an ounce of concern that I was supporting my family, and it was clear that the decision was final. She tapped a pencil on her desk as she looked at my nervous reaction. She didn't have a financial care in the world; in fact, even her office furnishings were the finest available, right down to the cushioned, three-inch-deep carpeting.

"I don't understand," I replied.

"Well, we've observed that you haven't been doing your duties lately. I guess it's mainly this Jesus stuff you're into. It seems you use your job as a religious bandwagon. We need a receptionist and not a preacher. The bulletin board stunt was the final blow. That made our mind up that we'd have to replace you. But we have a replacement and she'll be starting next week, so Saturday will be your last day. I'm sorry."

God, you're carrying out this trust business too far! I cried.

In less than three months' time, all my earthly security had been removed! We still had a roof over our heads, but it was "leaky," since we didn't know how we would make the expensive mortgage payment. My chaotic life style had really changed very little. However, I was sure that if Jesus was watching over the sparrows and the lilies of the field, he was surely keeping watch over the Atkinson family.

Again, in unbelievable succession, doors closed for Chip to find a job. Bills added up and grocery money had to be trimmed. It seemed as though I had just been through that whole scene in a different act of another play. I wavered between shaking my fist at God and trying to thank him in all circumstances. Chip finally learned of a stock firm that would hire him as a broker, but it would cost us $200 for the training. We scraped together the funds and learned on the starting day that he then had to purchase his own desk, telephone, and insurance, and the company insurance plan wouldn't cover me because I was an alcoholic.

It was a bad time for investments and more weeks went by in which we could buy only the necessities. Major bills accumulated and creditors justifiably called and wrote overdue notices. The car sat idle in the garage because we couldn't afford gasoline and repair bills. Worst of all, Mark, Ross, and Stephanie had to go without the luxuries their friends had. I simply waited and prayed for a miracle. I fought off thoughts that perhaps I had "jinxed" Chip. Lean weeks turned to months and we could barely afford life's necessities. Finally when we sank into the depths—at least financially—God lovingly reached down and provided for many of our needs through his incredible family! God's people rallied! We had joined the Edina Baptist Church in a suburb of Minneapolis, and it didn't take us long to realize that God's people are beautiful, caring people!

Ardys Schellenberg and Joey Northrup planned a surprise birthday party for me. Several women from the church attended and presented me with a check for $168. I accompanied another friend, Sharon West, as she went grocery shopping, watching with envy as she ran up a $95 bill for her family. She then handed those ten bags of groceries over to me!

Anonymous gifts arrived at our home signed simply: "Jesus loves you."

God had an uncanny way of communicating to my friend Polly Petry, the very item my family yearned for. Be it a pot roast or fresh strawberries, more than once Polly was compelled to purchase such items and bring them over. She could not explain the phenomenon but simply dropped the goods at my door while I stood frozen with amazement and gratitude to God and Polly!

I had to face the humiliation of food stamps and found it difficult to thank God for that humbling experience.

We found ourselves months behind on our house payment and Chip and I prayed for a miracle. We told no one, wanting to let God show himself to be a miracle-worker apart from friends. A week later our income-tax refund came in the mail. It was for the amount of the house payment, *plus* ten cents left over for postage!

We wrote down every bill we owed and turned them over to Jesus with a note: "Dear Jesus, these problems belong to you. We're releasing them now. Chip and Sandy."

How my heart broke as Ross handed us his bankbook and urged us to use the $120 he had saved over two years doing odd jobs. I could not accept it and prayed instead for a miraculous provision of $30 to buy Ross a watch for his birthday. The next day a leading department store called to say they had just discovered that I had a $30 credit on my account from five years earlier! They had given up finding me until that morning when the file card fell out and turned over, revealing a phone number where I could be reached!

How could I doubt God's love and concern for me and my family? He had complete control over the Atkinson home and cared about us right down to a birthday present for Ross! In his own time, he would bail us out of our situation in a way that would, no doubt, bring glory to him!

TWENTY
There's Mirth in Girth!

For fifteen years I had curbed and stifled my appetite with pills, liquor, and cigarettes. Now I had pulled the plug on all three and quickly gained 35 pounds. I was obsessed with my outward appearance, but God wanted to divert that attention toward inner beauty. I was certainly learning trust in a lot of areas, but could I possibly trust God with my weight, too? That seemed to be the final closet to be cleaned and the final chapter on self-indulgence that needed to be written—hopefully with a happy ending!

The scars of childhood obesity were engraved on my mind. At age nine I recalled how I was the fattest child on the block. I remembered the kids testing out a new swing that year. Their words rang through my mind: "If the swing will hold Sandy Smith, it will hold anybody!" I had gotten on the swing defiantly and moments later I had lain sprawled on the ground. It hadn't held me and I'd nearly broken the swing and my head!

But since going off the alcohol, Dexedrine, and cigarettes, I had become a sneaky eater. It wasn't unusual for me to get up at 3:00 A.M. to drink a whole can of chocolate sauce. By eating late at night or getting up in the middle of the night, I could then "sleep it off" and ease my conscience. But I couldn't "sleep it off" my figure, and as the inches added up I was tempted to take diet pills—which surely would have led to Dexedrine again. Gaining a victory over my uncontrollable desire to eat was as important as the deliverance I'd had from alcohol and pills.

I felt I needed a "halfway house" to help me learn self-control and proper eating habits. If I could be with others who had similar problems, I could gain the moral support I needed. An incident with my son Mark nudged me over what I saw as the line of no return, and forced me to seek help.

Mark had saved some money to buy him and his girl friend a chocolate cream pie, which cost him $3.50. He told me that we could all have a piece as long as we saved two big pieces for Jenny and him the next day. Four pieces were served for dinner that night, and the remaining two pieces were placed in the refrigerator for the next day.

That night, all I could think about was the chocolate cream pie in the refrigerator! At 2:00 A.M. I came down to the refrigerator and yielded to the gnawing temptation to eat a piece of it! That left only one piece. As I climbed back into bed, I had a hard time escaping my terrible guilt feelings. Eventually I buried my guilt and went back to sleep.

The next day Mark discovered that the pie was nearly gone. He was justifiably furious, for he had worked two hours to earn the money for it. I flatly denied eating the pie and said I had no idea who might have done it. Suddenly it occurred to me that I was pulling the same con-game with food that I had done with pills and liquor! I would lie and connive and cheat and even convince myself of my half-truths and lies. I was a slave to my desires and gave in to them at the expense of those closest to me. The walk down the stairs toward Mark's room was my longest mile, for I had to confess my lie to him. I prayed that God would somehow use my weight problem for his glory and help me to gain control over my obsession with food.

Shortly after, I heard of an organization called Overeaters Anonymous and I felt that perhaps this was the group that could give me the moral support and guidance I needed. It never occurred to me that I would be given an opportunity to share Jesus with forty women each week for the next four months.

Once a week we met for counsel and encouragement, and several times I was asked to share my testimony in front of the whole group, within our small groups, and on a one-to-one basis. I shared how Jesus had come into my life and had transformed me; how he had helped me break from alcohol, drugs, cigarettes, and a general self-indulgent life style.

Many of the women with whom I shared were Jewish, and beneath a hardened exterior at the mention of Jesus, I sensed a hunger for "spiritual food" within them. They confided in me about the spiritual emptiness they felt, and how the Jewish traditions of their parents or grandparents brought them little satisfaction. They had been told the usual lines about Jesus—that he was the cause of Jewish persecution and that it had been the Christians and followers of Christ that lighted the persecution fires and then fanned the flames. I carefully shared the Jewishness of Jesus and tried to show them that a true born-again Christian loves the Jew and deplores any kind of anti-Semitism or prejudice.

As the weeks passed more women began to trust me. One by one they would approach me at the meetings to ask further questions. I saw how God planted me in Overeaters Anonymous to be their local missionary and bring them the gospel of hope in Jesus.

The women tested my own convictions, too. Why couldn't God control my eating indulgences as he had the alcohol and drugs? If God was truly in control of my life, why did I still have a weight problem? I told them I felt that God allowed temptations in our lives, but then provided a way for us to have victory over those temptations. Often we had to be brought to a point where every other escape hatch failed us and only God could deliver us. I said we must recognize all such dependencies as sin and confess them to God, then allow the Holy Spirit to fill us with such a love for Jesus and for others that nothing else really matters. A hunger and a thirst for God and his Word had to replace all earthly hunger pains and cravings.

Could I practice what I preached? The women looked to me to see if I was a worthy public relations agent for the kingdom of God and Heaven! What a responsibility, but what incentive for me to work on the weight problem with God's help.

Slowly I began to lose weight, this time with no gimmicks. The more I lost, the more credibility my testimony to Jesus had and the more women sought me out.

Over that six-month period I shared Christ with dozens of women. I had the privilege of leading several of them to a saving knowledge of Jesus, and I know God used me to plant a seed in the lives of many more. But whatever area of our lives is producing spiritual fruit is sure to undergo special attack from Satan. The temptation to be a compulsive eater still raises its ugly head every day. I imagine it to be similar to the temptation in the Garden of Eden—just a bite of that forbidden food won't hurt. And yet one bite ushers in a whole host of sin, spiritual destruction, and self-hate, and eventually results in separation from God. No, he never leaves us, but our own self-inflicted disgust drives a wedge between us and we feel unworthy of his forgiveness.

Indeed there is no joy in zippers that zip

only halfway, buttons that won't button, and seams that must be let out. But when we look at the problem from God's point of view—and see that he is using it to build character, increase our trust in him, and give the ultimate victory to him, we can look back and say that perhaps there is, after all, just a little bit of mirth in girth!

TWENTY-ONE
Not Perfect— Only Forgiven

I constantly prayed for two things: opportunities to share Christ, and a solution to some of our financial problems. I never expected God to work in both areas simultaneously.

My friend Donna Lundborg introduced me to the craft of making antique books. The going price for a book was about fifteen dollars, and if I planned carefully I stood to make a good profit on each antique book I made. The books, which might have an inspirational thought or Bible passage on one side and a picture on the other, would sit open faced on a fireplace mantle or some other place of prominence in a home. The final process of shellacking and spraying with gold paint would preserve them practically forever.

I decided to go into the business of making the books, working out of my home. Early in this business adventure I made God my partner.

My reputation in the craft spread quickly and I became the leading distributor of the books in Minnesota. I made more than fifty of them a week and earned over $200 a week from their sale. Even Gerald Ford had an antique book of mine; other orders were filled as far away as Germany and Ireland.

God blessed the book business beyond my expectation, but I soon saw that the reason was more than financial. I saw that I had a responsibility that went beyond filling orders and paying bills. I was being a missionary to the hundreds with whom I came in contact—customers, gift store owners, and friends.

Then a whole new avenue opened up. The Salvation Army asked me to talk to the girls in their halfway house program—a live-in home for unwed mothers and women with drug and alcohol problems! The assignment was to show them the creative antique book craft, but God opened the door to show them the Creator of the universe. Although the staff members of the home were Christians, most of the girls in the home were not. Many were bitter, hardened, angry young women. As I shared the antique book craft with the girls, I was met with an audience of apathetic faces. They blew their cigarette smoke at me and stared out the window. None would give me the satisfaction of an ounce of interest.

I shot up an urgent prayer to Jesus to show me what to do. I was awkward and embarrassed and felt I could just as well be talking to the walls. But God seemed to guide me into sharing

my testimony, for it was a story all the young
women could identify with in one way or
another.

I stopped in the middle of the book demon-
stration, came to the front of the table, and sat
on the edge. I paused for several moments of
silence, hoping to capture their attention by
making things awkward for them, too. I looked
out over the dozen or more young girls and saw
on each of their faces the scars of a lifetime of
horror. Even at age sixteen or eighteen, they
knew the ugly side of life. They had fallen prey
to many of life's binding snares. Their hopeless
faces expressed that they did not believe there
was an alternative. Yes, they'd heard about
Jesus and the freedom and forgiveness he offers,
but they'd heard about him from those who
hadn't walked the same path they'd followed.
The counselors and staff members of the home
had the answers, all right, but their sheltered
backgrounds drove a giant-sized wall between
them and the girls and destroyed their
credibility.

"I know you think I've got my act all
together," I said slowly, "but I want you to
know I haven't and that I've faced all the
struggles you girls have faced. I'm an alcoholic
and at one time I was a drug addict. I lived
purely for selfish pleasures. I had no hope and
no purpose in living. I faced despair nearly every
day unless I drank a quart of alcohol and took
sixteen speed capsules. After I drove my
husband away from me I took a razor blade to
my wrist. But then I met Jesus."

I stopped; now I had all eyes on me. Behind their sunken, lifeless eyes there seemed to flicker a spark of hope, because someone else had crossed that line of despair.

I continued, speaking quietly and slowly. "Then I heard of a Man who would love me just as I am. That Man was Jesus. I didn't have to impress him with my intelligence or creativity or my good works. I simply had to trust him and give him my life, and ask him to transform it. I asked him to replace my selfish desires with a new love for others. For a long time I felt Jesus could never forgive me because I had done so many rotten things. But I read in the Bible that all we have to do is to confess those sins and we're forgiven. If we ask Jesus into our hearts and lives he will give us eternal life. I had no hope before I met Jesus. Had I not quit drinking I would have killed myself because I was destroying my liver. My nervous system was shattered nearly beyond repair from the drugs. But I'm standing up here this afternoon telling you that I am a new person because of Jesus."

No one moved and every eye was fastened on me. Because I had tasted the bitter dregs of worldly pleasures and sin, I knew my words had penetrated their hearts.

The girls wouldn't let me go home that afternoon, and for hours I shared the love of Jesus with them. As I left the home toward early evening God clearly impressed upon me that he had a special mission for me. He was calling me to be a messenger, proclaiming the only true liberator, Jesus, as the only one to free others from drugs, alcohol, and self-abuse. We can't do it through any program of our own. It is obtained through deliberately turning away from ourselves, toward God, and then inevitably toward others. With the love of Christ we are certainly not perfect, but definitely forgiven! Surrendering our time, comforts, and conveniences for the sake of one person who otherwise might not meet the life-changing Savior, is one of the most rewarding experiences of the Christian. There's no longer any need for various kinds of chemical-coping devices!

"I'll shout it from the mountain tops/I want my world to know/the Lord of love has come to me/I want to pass it on!" So goes the contemporary gospel song. So goes my heart!